"When life doesn't mirror our dreams, ___
sion, and escape. Tez speaks from his ___
help and no-fuss straight talk. With hur ___
ness, this easy-to-read book shines a lig___ ____ practical steps to embrace
God's mission for single-again dads."

Bill Hodgson
Former national director of Cru Australia

"*The Single Dad Detour* takes us along a journey that too many have traveled and where too few maps exist. Tez's narrative resonates and his authenticity is liberating. If I were a single parent on this journey, I'd want Tez's comforting voice on my GPS. It's a warm and understanding voice that's traveled the back roads and knows where it's going."

Rick James
Publisher for Cru Press, and author of *Jesus Without Religion* and
A Million Ways to Die

"For an easily overlooked demographic, Tez Brooks wisely, honestly, and courageously deep-dives into how divorced fathers can survive being single and still be really good dads. From inner work to practical steps, this book serves and 'skills up' the man who finds himself parenting outside the significant relationship of marriage."

Rohan Dredge
Founder and CEO of New Level Leadership, and senior pastor of
Discovery Church, Melbourne, Australia

"Honest, vulnerable, and often hilarious, Tez Brooks reveals the raw sorrows and transcendent joys of fatherhood after divorce. *The Single Dad Detour* is a graphic road map drawn from the personal experiences of single dads. Along this byway, in a comfortably conversational way, Brooks reveals unexpected signposts of scriptural wisdom collected from years of both crashed guardrails and triumphant victory laps."

Dr. Alan Kent Scholes
International speaker, theologian, and seminary professor for Cru's
Institute of Biblical Studies, and author of *Enjoying God*

"Single fathers are busy and often emotionally mangled. They need information like *The Single Dad Detour* that's easy to read and use. There's no delusion, only sincere assistance for men on this detour, offering real help to see them through."

Mike Klumpp
Solo parenting expert for Divorce Care Ministries, and author of
The Single Dad's Survival Guide

THE SINGLE DAD
DETOUR

THE SINGLE DAD DETOUR

DIRECTIONS FOR FATHERING
AFTER DIVORCE

TEZ BROOKS

Kregel
Publications

Dedicated to my amazing children:
Sharaya, Caleb, Jadyn, and Anicah.
You continue to inspire me.

Contents

Part Three—Caution: Men at Work

Acknowledgments

Special thanks
- To those faithful friends who came alongside me during my single parenting days. You blessed me and provided a safe environment for my children and me.
- To my church and to Cru, for your sound biblical teaching.
- To my friends at Word Weavers International (Orlando chapter): for your grace-filled critiques and encouragement to create the best for our Lord.
- To my editors, Sarah De Mey, Leslie Santamaria, and Cindy Huff. You make me look good.
- To all the men I interviewed who shared their sometimes painful stories in order to help me write this book.
- To Christine, my love. You believe in me. Thank you for sacrificing hundreds of hours without me in order to help some single dads you'll never meet.
- To my Heavenly Father—not only for saving and continually transforming me into the man you want me to be, but also for giving me a piece of your creative side. I'm amazed and devoted.

So Why a Book?

"I just want you out of my life!"

It was a Friday night when my wife blurted out that she was leaving me.

I suspected a breakup was imminent, but after almost a decade of marriage, I was hoping we could work it out.

Regardless of the fact that my wife turned from God and left me, I still had to face that I was not a great husband. Sin worked in *my* life as well—perhaps this drove my wife to the arms of another.

Within months it was over. Surveying the carnage open-mouthed, I was suddenly solo. I looked for help on the shelves of many a Christian bookstore and found little out there for single fathers. I learned a lot on my own and never dreamed of being at a place where I could actually turn and help others.

Now decades later—this book.

Because my life journey includes the hardship of an unwanted split, I wrote with the divorced father in mind. How do you raise children on your own, after the split? These pages were not written to help define who sinned and who is the innocent victim in a divorce. We have the Bible for that. What we will learn is how to be a rock for our kids while still healing from the trauma ourselves. Sadly, I have met several guys whose wife walked out on them and the kids to pursue a life unencumbered by the responsibility of having a family in tow.

Matthew Weinshenker, an assistant professor of sociology at Fordham University, said the state trend mirrors what's happening nationally, where the number of single dads has almost doubled from 1.5 million to 2.79 million since 1990.[1]

Although the topic of survival applies to widowers, never-married dads, and even mothers—I have written, from a Christian worldview, with the goal of helping divorced fathers in particular.

This book is about making life work for a father on his own. It's my hope the Holy Spirit will use my story, and those of other men, to minister to dads everywhere who desperately want to glorify God as they lead their precious ones through life.

Besides being a former youth pastor and police chaplain, I served in various ministry-related roles most of my adult life. I currently serve as a full-time missionary with Cru, an international ministry whose goal is to win, build, and send disciples. I'm not a licensed counselor, but it's with that ministry background that I'm able (with God's unbelievable grace) to offer some hope and wisdom for dads.

I also don't want to minimize the value of my marital experiences. Being divorced doesn't disqualify a person from giving solid, biblical marriage counsel to men. To the contrary, some of the best counsel I've heard has come from men who've journeyed through the back roads of divorce. Despite my past, I've seen how God-given wisdom has outshined any labels that religious judges have tried to attach.

Lastly, being the father of four brings lessons that are better shared than tucked away. I have two children from my previous marriage. Seven years after my ex-wife left, I married Christine, a lovely woman who daily lives out Proverbs 31. Together, we produced two more girls. God continues to use all four of my kids to develop me into the father he wants me to be.

My favorite Scripture passage says it best: "I'm not saying that I have this all together, that I have it made. But I am well on my way, reaching

out for Christ, who has so wondrously reached out for me. Friends, don't
get me wrong: By no means do I count myself an expert in all of this, but
I've got my eye on the goal, where God is beckoning us onward—to Jesus.
I'm off and running, and I'm not turning back" (Phil. 3:12–14 MSG).

PART 1

Driver's Education

CHAPTER 1

Where in the World Am I?
(Finding Your Way)

"I don't need a map; I'm just lost."

Her name was Babette—Babs for short. She talked a lot and was a little bossy, but I could overlook that. Slim and eye-catching, Babs took me places I never dreamed of. I couldn't keep my hands off her, even when I was driving. She was my first Global Positioning System (GPS), and I loved turning her on.

She told me how far I needed to go, and when I would arrive at my destination. Her British accent captivated me. After all, I was accustomed to a female voice always telling me what to do—but that's a book of another title.

I became dependent upon Babs. She was amazing—I didn't have to think about anything. She even knew where all the seedy little places were. Places you don't want people to know you're going—like Goodwill and Taco Bell.

After a few years, though, I noticed I couldn't always trust her. At times she seemed a bit confused and disoriented, recalculating for no reason at all. I updated her maps and kept her from extreme temperatures, but once she made the decision to shut down, I couldn't stop her. One day, Babs broke beyond repair. Our relationship was over and I felt—lost.

Grabbing an old atlas from under my car seat, I was able to navigate to my destination—old school. This method wasn't as convenient as Babs, but it got me there. In a similar manner, my experience as a single parent found me lacking. Sharaya was only six and Caleb was four, when the tragedy of divorce touched their little lives. Despite my best efforts, I couldn't protect my daughter and son from its wounds.

YOU MATTER

"Whatever you think about and feel as you reflect, remember that you play a pivotal role in your child's life. You do make a difference. You are tremendously important in the life of your child."
—Carey Casey, CEO, National Center for Fathering[1]

They were forever changed—their journey forever altered.

My Journey

My first wife and I entered our marriage with some major issues from our past, none of which had been properly addressed, diagnosed, treated, or resolved.

Early on, the warning signs in our relationship began to show. Impurity stained our union both before and after the wedding. Forgiving one another, we pressed on. My faith in God ran deep, but I quickly saw we were headed down two different roads to find the restoration we needed.

Attempts to make repairs using date nights, prayer times, marriage retreats, and counseling didn't help. I prayed for a miracle. My desire was to woo my wife back, but when I begged, it only made me look pathetic—it disgusted her.

After months of prayer, counsel, even shameless begging, it dawned on me I couldn't *make* her love me. Like my GPS, the relationship fell apart and I was quickly lost.

This crossroad led to a decision. A few weeks after our separation, I had to stop and regroup. Eating cups of noodles and renting movies every night wasn't good. Wallowing in my self-pity had to stop. It was time to man-up and help my children walk through this.

I found myself in much the same situation as when I'm driving in a new area without a map. The convenience of two people working together to navigate through parenthood was gone.

Back then, I had no older men speaking into my life—even my father didn't know how to counsel me. He was a solid Christian who loved the Lord and raised me in church—even leading me to Christ. Yet my dad declined giving fatherly guidance even when I would ask him outright. Perhaps it was fear of giving poor counsel, or maybe because his own parents never guided him. At any rate, by the time I turned sixteen I was on my own when it came to finding wisdom during challenging circumstances. It was a time before accountability partners were in vogue. So when my marriage failed, I was already used to being an island and too naïve to seek out a mentor.

The next few months following the separation were full of complicated decisions about my identity, my fatherhood, my integrity, and more. Did people still consider me a respectable married man? Where did I fit in?

In a gospel tract I helped create with Cru, I share my journey of faith. I felt like I was always God's problem child—as if he felt obligated to make me his own, just because I repented of my sins. Through my childhood and college years, there was an underlying belief that if God had the choice, he would rather have skipped over me.

As an adult, I built my life on the dream that a wife, kids, and a house would make me successful. That dream fell apart when I lost everything that brought me security. I felt worthless, belonging to no one. Rejection paralyzed me. Although I was a Christian, I wasn't fully trusting in Christ. I couldn't see my true identity as his child.

There were more concerns. How was I to handle the slander against my wife? Attitudes, bad choices, and even outright sin both angered and embarrassed me. Lies, accusations, fraud, and even jail time touched our family. Do I ignore it or defend her honor in light of a possible reconciliation? It was only fair to let some know about my own sins, which may or may not have caused my wife to leave. It was all so untidy and somewhat disconcerting. At times I felt like I was watching an episode of Jerry Springer. It seemed daily there were moments when I had to make split-second decisions to take the high road or the low one. Unfortunately, if my kids were not around, the low road won out more than a few times.

Couple all this with the added feat of keeping life normal for Sharaya and Caleb—I was bound to drop the ball from time to time.

Killing Fatalism

Perhaps you're thinking about giving up. Maybe you're so tired you're starting to believe it's best to just leave it all behind—kids and all. You may have bought the lie that your children are better off with just a mother and in time they will resiliently forget about you. On the contrary, according to The Art of Manliness.com, kids growing up without a dad present are more likely to:

- Need constant approval to feel validated
- Have difficulty with assertiveness
- Lack confidence and self-esteem, especially in decision making
- Become harsh self-critics
- Value loyalty of friends to the exclusion of common sense
- Have difficulty finishing what they start
- Blame others rather than take responsibility[2]

The world may try to polish over the ugliness of divorce. These days it's considered derogatory to say "broken home," so we often hear that phrase replaced with a politically correct phrase like "single-parent environment." But let's face it, we're men—let's put on our big-boy pants and call it what it is. Divorce is ugly and depressing. It destroys families and God hates it. Now that we've admitted divorce requires a rebuilding of our lives after the smoke clears, hopefully we can talk openly, at times even humorously, about its effects on us dads.

I often encounter men who are in various places on the single-dad journey, without a map, like I was. They drift from one roadside attraction to another without direction, letting life's highway take them and their children wherever it wants.

Don't get me wrong—at times I too drifted. I still do sometimes. We don't always have a chance to direct the route life takes us. Despite this, we can still redirect our path with God's help, and if need be, pull into a rest area in order to reestablish a game plan.

It's essential to remember none of this caught God off guard. He is all-knowing. Even as you and I were exchanging vows with our respective wives, he was aware our families would be torn apart by our sins or another's. Before we were conceived he knew this. Yet in his sovereignty, God looked down through history and specifically chose us to be a daddy. The Lord can equip us to lead our children through this wilderness. He's put a lot of faith in us and he's the ultimate strategic planner. That encourages me.

YOU'RE NOT ALONE

"It was the early 1970s and I was recently divorced. I had three kids and was totally broke. I managed to find work back east on the straw-hat circuit—summer stock—but couldn't afford hotels, so I lived out of the back of my truck, under a hard shell."
—William Shatner[3]

Lead On

Although we can nurture quite well at times, men have been created with special abilities to organize and lead teams, hunt, and compete with courage and stamina. Dads can encourage their children to never quit—to press on, building confidence like no one else. Stepping up to polish those traits is key if we are to fulfill our role as fathers, especially during moments of crisis or prolonged seasons of change.

Circumstances like divorce may try to detour us, but we never want to embrace a fatalistic attitude about parenting the little ones God entrusted to our care. Call yourself a tiger dad, an overachiever, or a control freak—no matter. I believe the Lord calls all fathers to avoid abdicating leadership and to cast off lethargy in order to protect our kids from being devoured by the enemy and the world.

My hope is that this book will offer a little assistance for fathers trying to navigate through some pretty tough roadblocks. Therapist and *Huffington Post* writer, Emily Gordon says:

In my experience as a therapist and as a friend, it seems that the majority of the breakup resources available are for women and not men. Women, who tend to be more vocal about their emotional struggles, are the squeaky wheels that get the grease from friends, from online communities, from books, and from therapeutic approaches. Women are encouraged to go on an emotional journey of self-care after a divorce, while men are expected to need help learning how to cook and parent on their own. When you Google "how men handle divorce," many of the links advise women on what to do if their husbands become violent during the divorce process. Why is there so little focus on how men can heal after a divorce?[4]

Been There

Remarried years ago, I've placed the difficult season of single parenting behind me. I'm glad it is over. Some have suggested I make good use of my experience, but reliving it in order to help other dads seemed painful. Have you ever had a doctor poke around on some scar tissue you developed? Don't you just want to smack him? That's what I thought this would feel like. Writing a book to benefit others seemed as if I were digging in nasty cat litter to find someone else's car keys.

My flesh says, "Why should I have to dig through that for someone else? I found my own keys years ago."

But when the Holy Spirit works in me, he changes things. He has to come along and ruin everything—softening my heart and giving me supernatural compassion, which doesn't normally exist in me. It's the Spirit of God who moves me to gladly sift through the cat litter of life, clean up the car keys, and present them to those who can't seem to get where they need to go.

During the seven years I was between marriages, I served as custodial parent and other times noncustodial. Sometimes the kids and I lived in the same city, then other periods they resided out of state and we saw each other only once or twice a year.

Through it all, I never lost faith in God. I ran to him and haven't regretted it. Sharaya and Caleb survived, growing up into two fine adults. They share my opinion that none of us could have made it without God's help.

In John 12:32 Jesus says, "And I, when I am lifted up from the earth, will draw all people to myself." I want to lift him up in this book because I believe none of us can successfully make this journey without help from the Creator of the universe. Therefore, I reference him often. In fact, if you enjoy an interactive experience, I've included questions, scriptural references, and practical ideas at the end of each chapter. Hopefully, whether through prayer, journaling, or Scripture memorization, these will encourage you to develop a deeper relationship with God Almighty.

If you're a single dad, chances are you're trying to squeeze in a chapter here or there. Take time to do the interactive sections in a way that makes this more than just another book to read. Allow it to challenge, encourage, and refresh you. Your life is hard enough without the pressure to perform. Just love your kids well and love God more.

The Lord desires men who will rise to their potential in whatever situation they are facing, so the name of Jesus can be lifted up. Chances are good you're one of those men. So climb in, buckle your seat belt, and take a ride with me as we consider this unpredictable road you're traveling.

CHECKING YOUR GAUGES

Why am I reading this book?

What are some of the ways I drift when parenting?

Finish this sentence: "I lead my child best in the area of . . ."

Do I consider myself a Christ follower? Why or why not?

STUDYING THE MAP

"For I know the plans I have for you, declares the LORD, plans for welfare and not for evil, to give you a future and a hope." Jeremiah 29:11

REROUTING

Hug your kid(s).

Commit to making time at the end of each chapter to do the exercises provided. A blank journal will come in handy for some of these.

Try to give yourself equal portions of grace and discipline as you navigate through this season of life.

REFUELING

Lord, thank you for trusting me with the child you gave me. Help me lead him or her through this season well. Without you, I am lost. You have created me to be strong, but help me not to depend on my own know-how. Teach me to put my trust in you. I need you to show me the way. Amen.

CHAPTER 2

Who's Driving?
(Giving God Control)

"Jesus, don't take the wheel!"

I hate carpools. Agreeing to share a ride to work means giving up control to some degree—especially if I'm not the driver. After all, what if I want to grab a coffee at the drive-thru, or leave work early? Because I like to rule my own world, there have been times when I decided to forego the camaraderie of a shared ride just to be the one in charge.

Trying to manage parenting on our own is a lot like driving around town. When driving, we encounter self-imposed stressors like the radio, conversations with our passengers, the temperature in the car, the GPS chatting at us. The coffee cup in the console tempts us to take a sip: the ding-ding of a new text and that outdated Bart Simpson ringtone we keep forgetting to change—all demand our attention.

We also have outside stimuli. Aggressive drivers whip in and out of the lanes. Traffic cones, school zones, and potholes mock us, along with a million traffic signs, which we must immediately recognize by shape and color and then obey. Sometimes it's raining.

All is chaos, but we're in control, and *that's* the problem. All is chaos *because* we're in control.

The Coup

Although it may seem contradictory to the previous chapter, a key element of being a courageous and proactive leader for your family is to relinquish control to another—but not just anyone. I'm talking about God.

FURTHER STUDY

Cru has great articles about walking in the power of the Holy Spirit. Look for the "Train and Grow" tab at www.Cru.org for Bible studies on giving God full control of your life.

Surrendering control is an ongoing battle for me. Being the youngest child of tired, older parents, I learned to work out my problems on my own, without bothering anyone. They meant well, but my family of origin unwittingly affirmed independence as a desirable trait. Some childhood bullies and fair weather friends reinforced that I could not rely on people in certain situations. This has at times hindered my dependence on God.

In her article "Trusting," *Focus on the Family* magazine writer Shana Schutte says:

> When we try and take the wheel away from God because we don't trust Him, it will lead to emotional and spiritual fatigue. Why? Because we're doing something that we weren't created for. God made us to lean on him in dependence—to let him drive—which leads to contentment, and the confidence that we are exactly where we need to be, doing what we need to do, and fulfilling the role he created us for. This will usher in deep contentment.[1]

When we become Christians we are, in essence, giving up the directing of our lives. Before we prayed to receive Jesus, we were sitting on the thrones of our lives—making decisions, running our lives, controlling the direction we took. At some point we realized this wasn't working. Either by logic, a disaster, or some other event, we're drawn to Christ and the realization that our soul is in danger, that we need a Savior. So we repent, accept his forgiveness, and slide off the throne so Jesus can take residence there.

Recalcitrant by nature, it doesn't take long for our hearts to form a coup and reclaim that place of authority. We keep slipping up on that fancy seat again and booting Jesus back onto the floor. We then find our goals, priorities, and responsibilities in bedlam once again.

I need to be deliberate in chasing after and killing my pride and self-reliance. Without Christ I can do nothing. I might try to fix circumstances on my own. It might even work out OK. However, this isn't biblical and it doesn't reflect a heart of trust or reliance on God. Each time I try to move in my own know-how, what I'm basically saying is, "God, I don't really believe you can help me. Give me the wheel; I can do it better." The driving force of that mind-set is fear—fear that God won't help us or fear of what others are thinking.

I faced several trials as a single dad: financial hardships, social adjustments, medical emergencies, and arguments with the mother of my children. When challenged, my need to control kicked in, to protect my little family from the realities of life. Failing and desperate for change, I fell at God's feet.

The driver's seat was not where I belonged, so I let God chauffeur. But that was another mistake. A chauffeur drives, but he's still not in control. I was sitting in the back seat, barking orders to God. What a ruse.

I finally learned that a life directed by God was necessary to get through difficulties. This was the only way to be the man of God—the father—he wanted me to be. Still, from time to time I attempt some backseat driving.

I Got This

We men are fixers, after all. We like to repair situations. It's part of our DNA, but at times it gets us in hot water with our wives, mothers, and children. Nonetheless, rather than learning to be an empathetic listener, we continue trying to mend things. It makes us feel good about ourselves to have accomplished something—to help improve the world or an individual. I tried to renovate my daughter's attitude without the Lord's help one embarrassing holiday.

Christmas shopping can be stressful on a guy. It seems like I'm forever trying to hold on to something while shopping. I'm trying to hang on to my coat, my shopping cart, my sanity. Then there's everyone else asking me to hold things.

"Hold my hand, Daddy."

"Hold my purse, Daddy."

"Hold your horses, Sir. The checkout line starts back there."

Are you kidding? I can barely hold my bladder.

After one of these particularly joyous shopping excursions, I forgot to hold one of the most important things—my tongue.

We were on the freeway, my kids and I. We were trying to rush home for yet another neighborhood party. If I could get home with time to spare, we might be able to toss some frozen mini-quiches in the oven. Then we could slip into those kitschy red sweaters we have and walk down to the Browns' for a painful night of eggnog and dips.

Don't get me wrong, the dips were nice, and they had a beautiful home.

In the back seat, my daughter began whimpering because she didn't get to see Santa at the mall. I ignored it, trying to pay attention to the immense holiday traffic.

In front of us, a fir tree on wheels was traveling at the breakneck speed of thirty miles per hour, a reminder of yet another thing to buy before Christmas Eve. The other two lanes were filled with cars zipping past us like hummingbirds in a hurricane. It was unlikely I'd be changing lanes anytime soon.

As I crept along the interstate, anxiety about decorating a tree set in. Finances were tight. *Paper chains and popcorn strands might be my only option this year.*

Suddenly, the fussing from the back seat got louder, turning into a cry. She was obsessing over St. Nick. I remember seeing Santa in the center of the mall, complete with a candy cane throne, but hurried past him. I was not about to spend a hundred dollars on photos of my daughter sitting in a stranger's lap.

"I wanna see Santa!" the screaming continued. As always, she insisted on pulling others into her little drama.

I'd listened to the whining long enough. Blood rushed to my temples like magma. Unable to hold my temper any longer, the day's activities carried me cruelly to this Mt. Saint Helens moment. I yelled into the rearview mirror, "That's enough! Santa's dead!"

As soon as the words left my mouth, I knew I had messed up. What could I do? The words were out there, stinging my daughter's heart like a giant bar of soap in the eyes of childlike reverie and imagination.

My little darling began wailing, "Nooo, Santa's not dead, is he?"

I sighed, slinking low in the driver's seat. Minimizing is always my first defense. So, to look unconcerned about the blunder, I pretended to check my side mirrors for traffic—anything to appear nonchalant. Inside I was kicking myself.

I supposed I could forget any Father-of-the-Year award.

For the next twenty minutes the cries of a broken heart flooded the vehicle. I wanted to cry too, as the Holy Spirit excavated my heart.

When we got home, I took my daughter aside, hugged her, and asked forgiveness for being such a grinch. Apologizing to my child was a good lesson in humility for me. Far from the perfect father, this wouldn't be the last time I lost it or said something I regret. That night I started a splendid habit of saying "I'm sorry" when I blow it with my kids. It would prove an invaluable tool in sustaining my authenticity as the spiritual leader in our home.

For my little girl, my apology and admission of wrong was her tree topper for the night. She sank into my arms as we sat in her room snuggling, while *Silent Night* played from the stereo. We were having a moment.

I had spent the day holding things I didn't want to. Now I was holding something I never wanted to let go of. Needless to say, we were a bit late for the Browns' party. That's OK; those dips could wait.

Lance, Dean, and Billy Ray

Sometimes we try to fix things in a few seconds, the result of which takes years to reverse. Lance was twenty-six when he became a single dad. His son, Kyle, was six. The breakup was hard on everyone. Lance particularly found it difficult not being in his son's life every day. One afternoon, while playing with friends, Kyle wet himself. Lance was furious. Already stressed out, he tried to fix a deeper matter by addressing only the external symptom.

MOBILE STATS

1 in 3 teens text more than 100 times daily.[2]

30% of 17-year-olds have received a sexually explicit text.[3]

20% have sent nude or semi-nude photos of themselves.[4]

48% agree that parents overreact to this.[5]

"I disciplined him in a way I am not proud of," admits Lance. "I was struggling with being only a part-time parent, and I took it out on my son. Afterward, the Lord reminded me how hurt and confused Kyle was from the divorce. How he might be wondering if he was losing me because I moved out. If Kyle was questioning my love for him, the harsh punishment probably solidified his fears. I apologized, but from then on I felt I needed to overcompensate by showing my son how much I really did love him."

Fortunately, Lance had the ears to hear from God and repair the relationship with his son. Dean wasn't so insightful. His daughter was fourteen when she came to live with him. When he found out she had developed an Internet friendship with a thirty-year-old man, Dean remained calm. Without a word, he installed software that blocked Kyleen from using the web. Then he deleted her social networks. Dean fixed the problem on his own without seeking the Lord for wisdom. Soon after, Kyleen moved back to her lenient mother, who allowed the cyber relationship to continue.

Who won?

It's this same desire to fix things that gets in the way of my dependence on God. Looking for help from my education or experience is not the answer. Although I encourage looking to a godly community for help, even this is not the answer. Psalm 91:2 says, "I will say of the LORD, 'He is my refuge and my fortress, my God, in whom I trust'" (NIV).

We've talked about getting control of our life, and we talked about letting God have control. There is also a third school of thought—denial.

When we are in denial that any control at all needs to happen, we ignore things we should actually be praying about.

In a March 2011 interview with *GQ* magazine, Billy Ray Cyrus, when asked about his daughter Miley's reckless behavior, said, "I should have been a better parent. I should have said, 'Enough is enough—it's getting dangerous and somebody's going to get hurt.'" He continued, "I should have, but I didn't. Honestly I didn't know the ball was out of bounds until it was up there in the stands somewhere."[6]

Sadly, we can be a lot like Billy Ray in any area of our lives. If we don't get the control we want, we rebel by choosing to deny a solution is needed. So how do we find the balance between being too passive and micromanaging, both of which can land us in the ditch? We'll explore this in the next chapter.

CHECKING YOUR GAUGES

What triggers control issues in you?

In what ways have you tried to fix your broken family on your own?

In what ways do you react during stressful seasons in your life?

Are these reactions healthy or harmful?

STUDYING THE MAP

"The LORD is close to the brokenhearted and saves those who are crushed in spirit. The righteous person may have many troubles, but the LORD delivers him from them all." Psalm 34:18–19 (NIV)

REROUTING

Habits of self-reliance are not easily broken. Make a list of at least five things you are currently trying to fix on your own. Lift this list to the sky and ask God to take the responsibility for all those issues—to care for you. For accountability purposes, share this list with a trusted friend. Ask him to follow up with you and see if you continue to grow in the area of dependence on God.

REFUELING

God, I want you to be Lord of everything in my life. Too often I am self-directed and push you out of the way. Jesus, take the chaos of my life and bring organization and order to my family. Help me be the man of God and the father you desire me to be, in Jesus's name. I'm sliding over, God—you drive. Amen.

CHAPTER 3

The Engine Lights
(Recognizing Warning Signs)

"It's just the engine; we're fine."

I was nineteen—old enough to know better. My yellow Maverick was a clunker and needed more attention than I was willing to give. In a hurry to get to work, I cranked the engine, threw the car into reverse, checked my mirrors, and backed out into the street. I popped in my favorite Hall and Oates tunes and raced through town. I never saw the engine light flashing. Over the music, I never heard the steady *ding, ding, ding.* However, once I got on the highway, I noticed the smoke pouring out from under the hood. By then it was too late. The engine block had cracked. I learned a valuable lesson that day—glance at my dashboard from time to time.

Ten years later, my friend Rick was making a similar mistake. He was overlooking the warning signals of an impending disaster. Rick had venom in his voice: "It takes eighty percent of my paycheck for child support. I have to move in with my sister. It's not right, man. It's oppressive. I'm already two months behind and my ex is complaining that she can't afford school supplies for Heather."

I had to pity Rick. Society might call him a deadbeat dad, but they didn't know all the facts. He had been a decent Christian father for years. He brought up his daughter in church, attended her recitals, clothed and fed her well. But when his marriage ended, he found himself paying a mortgage for a house he no longer lived in and giving court-ordered child support far above the standard of living he had provided for his daughter prior to the divorce. "What are the courts using to calculate that amount?" Rick spat.

Over the following months I saw him become bitter and resentful toward his ex-wife as well as the courts. When he turned to his church for moral support, he was met with indifference. After a while he stopped going to church. He began drinking and visiting his daughter less and less. Rick was arrested on a DUI, was fired from his job, and lost all visitation rights with his daughter.

ARE YOU A DEADBEAT?

According to the U.S. Department of Health and Human Services, the following are **not** deadbeat dads:

- Those dads unable to pay the normal support.
- Those dads who made financial arrangements with the mom outside of court.
- Those dads who never received a court order to pay.

Of the 10 million custodial mothers not getting support, only 7% of those are because of a true deadbeat situation.[1]

His trouble wasn't the lack of income. It wasn't the fault of Rick's ex-wife or his church. It wasn't even his drinking. The root issue was that Rick refused to stop and look at the warning sign. He never checked his dashboard to see that his forgiveness gauge was in the red. Had Rick noticed this issue early on and prayed about it, he might have been able to avoid the ultimate disaster of losing his daughter.

Breaking Dad

I don't care how godly we think we are, when men go through a marital breakup, we experience—like Rick—temptations we never struggled with before. The pain of rejection can drive us to slander, property damage, pathetic begging, alcohol, withholding alimony, or rebounding with other women. We should never let our need to feel attractive and desirable lead us to places that will embarrass us later. It just makes the entire male gender look bad.

Speaking of women, boundaries with your ex-wife can get pretty gray in the midst of a breakup. There's breakup sex and make-up sex and everything in between. You'll have folks sharing all kinds of differing opinions about what is or isn't allowed when it comes to

BATTLE PLAN FOR PURITY

To learn more about overcoming the bondage of sexual sins, check out conquerseries.com.

intimacy. The phrase "still married in God's eyes" is thrown around a lot, but we need to keep our wits about us. Let me make it plain for you—it's not OK to make love to your ex-wife.

If the divorce has happened, then she is no longer your wife. Period.

Now if God restores your marriage and you get back together, that's wonderful! Begin courting your ex-wife at once and follow through with a proposal and a new marriage license. Until then, stay away from her bedroom. You can't skip these steps just because you used to be married to her.

I don't care how amorous you and your ex feel in the heat of the moment, don't complicate things. You might think you'd never dream of talking yourself into a passionate connection, especially after all the arguments and fighting. But there can be a magnetism between ex-spouses, because of the years of intimacy you experienced, which blinds you momentarily to all reason.

Guys, we've all been there hundreds of times since puberty. Whether you're struggling to look away from pornography or your neighbor jogging by the house, it's that moment when you've allowed your imagination to go places it shouldn't. Now your head is swooning with desire and you can't think straight. Like Edward Cullen at a blood drive, you almost feel aggressive, unable to control your urges as they surge through your body.

Let's call it what it is. Bottom line—you're horny.

Whether it's your ex-spouse or a woman you're dating—stop it! Let's be men of honor. If she is not legally married to you, treat her like your sister.

According to the Bible, sex is for married couples only. It's a holy act ordained by the Lord, to be saved for the marital bed. Sex with someone who is not your spouse defiles both your bodies. It's an unholy act that breaks the heart of Jesus. Paul wrote about this in his letter to Corinth.

First Corinthians 6:18–20 says, "Flee from sexual immorality. All other sins a person commits are outside the body, but whoever sins sexually, sins against their own body. Do you not know that your bodies are temples of the Holy Spirit, who is in you, whom you have received from God? You are not your own; you were bought at a price. Therefore honor God with your bodies" (NIV).

A few years after my own divorce, both kids were living with me full-time. I made the mistake of allowing my ex-wife to stay at my house for a few weeks because she was homeless. Because of my strong persuasion that Christian singles should never live together, I would never have taken in a single woman in that situation, so why should my ex be any different?

Depleting all other options first, I offered to keep the kids but had no alternative housing arrangements for her. With all the history we shared, it was hard to turn away the mother of my children, especially in front of the kids. Against my better judgment, I took her in also, knowing she'd be a free sitter for the kids while I was at work.

Although nothing happened between us, it was a dim-witted move. After a week, I decided to take a vacation out of town, in order to get away from her. Even though I no longer had feelings for her, I didn't want to place myself in the line of temptation. Besides, it was confusing our kids and our friends. She moved out within two weeks, but people still whispered about it. Despite the propriety, my reputation suffered a slight setback—not to mention the false hope and confusion my kids experienced.

My point is, don't be an idiot. Be wary of placing yourself in the way of temptation or even the appearance of evil. When we're on emotional roller coasters, we're going to discover opportunities to make dumb decisions. We don't have to act on them, especially if we ask the Holy Spirit for wisdom and keep our spiritual engine lights in view.

Many times we innocently place ourselves in these situations. In the Old Testament, Joseph ran from Potiphar's wife when she tried to seduce him. Even with an upright heart, his reputation still got ruined. While he

sat in jail, I wonder if he contem-
plated how he might have better
avoided the incident.

The most important aspect
of giving God control is talking
with him all through the day,
seeking his guidance on decisions you have to make.

HOW DUMB ARE WE?

According to a survey by
Cleveland's WZAK radio station,
three in ten people end up having sex with their former spouse.[2]

I wish I were known as a man of prayer, but I don't seek God's advice
nearly enough. Praying about things helps us gauge our responses to circumstances. The Holy Spirit is able to step in and guide us—or even flash
a warning light—if we're hard of hearing.

I'm not saying you need to micromanage your every move with prayer.
If you need to use the restroom, use it. No need to check in with God on
that.

Grapefruit and Gas

One Christmas, some relatives gave me a grapefruit tree for my small
back yard in Florida. It was just a sapling. They made no attempt to hide
their motive, explaining they wanted fruit when they visited.

I had a little problem with that. It was more for *their* pleasure than
mine.

I thanked them with a smile, but inside I was not excited at all. I hated
grapefruit. I pictured myself spending resources I didn't have. It would
take a lot of time and money fertilizing and watering this little tree. It
could be years before seeing any fruit. If it did finally yield, I imagined
rats invading my property as they fed off the produce. I saw myself picking up the fallen, rotting fruit each week before I could mow the yard. I
just knew it would not end well for me.

Nevertheless, I planted it. Then that same night, I snuck outside and
drowned the roots with gasoline. Ignoring the threat of a hefty fine, I did
that for three nights, until I saw the leaves wither and die.

I know—I'm a coward and I'm stupid. But hey, I fixed the problem!

Now how easy would it have been to just be honest with the person who gave me the tree? Politely refusing the gift would have been OK in this situation. Better yet, I could have just planted the tree and prayed about it. I could have asked God to help me care for the tree and bless others with it. I could have addressed my sinful heart issues with maturity and turned the trial into a blessing. I ignored the Holy Spirit's warning lights.

Today I love grapefruit. I wish I had that tree in my yard now. It was a missed opportunity, all because I didn't pray. I tried to fix it on my own.

As a young man, I often forgot to add the oil of gladness to the squeaks that annoyed me. I also forgot to filter my decisions through prayer or take time for something as simple as refueling. Sometimes the engine light was flashing like crazy, but I was too busy staring into my rearview mirror, fixating on things I should have released to God.

Some of us never learn to depend on the Lord through trials. Like my friend Rick, we often expect the church to save us. Humans will let us down, and, if we're not careful, anger can grab a foothold in our hearts. If the bitterness is unchecked, a crisis can occur. I want to reiterate how imperative it is we turn to Christ for our help. It's prayer, not passivity, that gives us the balance of being proactive while still allowing God to lead us. When we let Christ drive us, then the Holy Spirit convicts and warns us of any impending failure.

CHECKING YOUR GAUGES

How often do you check your spiritual engine lights? What is your initial response when things spin out of control?

When are you most prone to fixing things yourself?

How do you keep an eye on your own spiritual engine lights?

Search your heart for any speck of bitterness toward your ex-wife, family members, church friends, and God. What is God revealing to you?

STUDYING THE MAP ————————————————————

> "Search me, God, and know my heart; test me and know my anxious thoughts. See if there is any offensive way in me, and lead me in the way everlasting." Psalm 139:23–24 (NIV)

REROUTING ————————————————————————

Sometimes we can be oblivious of how often we pull people into our negative experiences against their will. Do you have a friend who seems indifferent or even avoids time with you? Try to think the best of them first. Be prepared to accept that you may be pushing them away. If we talk too much about our troubles, others might find us miserable to be around. Be sensitive to the fact that others often can't relate nor find the grace to walk through our trials with us. Jesus will.

REFUELING ————————————————————————

> Father, help me pay attention to the warning signs. Holy Spirit, speak loudly to me when I'm distracted. Jesus, I commit to fixing my eyes on what's ahead, not my past. I've made mistakes, but that doesn't dictate who I am. Forgive my pride and help me pursue humility. Amen.

CHAPTER 4

A Fork in the Road
(Making Right Choices)

"Siri, where can I hide a body?"

Apart from my spouse having a terminal illness or accident, being a single dad never invaded my wildest imaginations. I came from a long line of Christians involved in ministry. Because of such a godly heritage, I never considered divorce would touch my family. I had been taught that God hates divorce and couples can work through anything with Christ's help. My plan was to raise the kids in an environment of faithful Christ followers. Then we'd spend our golden years spoiling the grandkids and organizing large family reunions. I assumed I'd grow old with the wife of my youth—sitting gray-haired on a front porch swing, reminiscing about the decades of our life together.

That dream began to dissolve when my wife walked away from the Lord and filed for divorce. In an attempt to be honorable, I moved out and let her stay in our house. As my life tumbled amidst lawyer consultations and apartment hunting, I comforted my children and continued hoping for reconciliation.

My manhood and self-worth challenged, nightmares of my wife with other men interrupted my sleep. During the day, I was consumed with thoughts of my kids climbing into another man's lap, enjoying a better life with a guy who had won them over somehow. I imagined him moving into my home and kissing my children good night. In these counterproductive imaginations he was younger, stronger, richer, and better looking than I could ever be. I couldn't keep my thoughts captive, and it ate away at me.

Choices

My crisis reached critical mass one Sunday night. My daughter, my son, and I had had a great weekend together, and I was returning them to their mother. As I arrived, I noticed the lights were out. Although her car was there, no one seemed to be home. We parked, and I decided to call her. *Perhaps she had walked over to a neighbor's house for a moment.*

WHEN THE EX OFFENDS

1. Close your eyes and count to twenty.
2. Don't send that e-mail until tomorrow, after you have cooled off.
3. Ask yourself if it will matter a year from now. If not, don't bother.
4. Put yourself in her shoes for a moment. Do you know all the facts?
5. Pray: Ask God for wisdom.

Before I could find her number, a black convertible pulled up to the curb. The passenger door opened, and the interior light revealed my wife and the driver inside—a handsome, much younger man. Not yet noticing us, she leaned over and kissed him, got out, then waved good-bye. In a flash, he was gone. She turned, noticed my vehicle, and froze.

What just happened?

My jaw dropped as I sat in the darkness of my vehicle. In these months leading up to our court date—even with the nightmares—I remained hopeful that we'd be able to salvage our marriage. I never considered my fears might materialize even before the divorce was final. *Did this jerk know she was still my wife? How dare he?* My stomach hurt and my throat went dry. I was trembling and getting tunnel vision.

My son saw it all. "Who was that, Daddy?"

The question snapped me out of my stupor. "I don't know, but you and your sister need to go—Mommy's here." I rushed them out of the car without saying good-bye and squealed the tires as I left. I wanted to catch that guy.

In the rearview mirror of my banged-up minivan, I saw my wife and children standing in the middle of the front yard in confusion. Tears welled up in my eyes and began to drop as I beat my fists against the steering wheel. Then I screamed out, "What is this? What are you doing, God? Do you even *know* what you're doing?"

This home wrecker could only be a few blocks ahead of me. Through my tears, I could hardly see to drive. As I gained on him, I was uncertain exactly what I would do when I caught up. Scenarios ran through my head—maybe at a red light I would run up to his vehicle with a crowbar and start breaking his headlights. Then I'd pull him out of the car and punch his face over and over again until no one could recognize him. Perhaps I'd take the high road and, like a gentleman, calmly ask him to leave my wife alone. Maybe I'd even share the gospel with him . . . or just kick him right in the crotch! Yeah, the low road seemed more fulfilling.

As I turned a corner, I saw him only a few blocks ahead of me—in that stupid convertible. *How impractical.* He slowed, and, ignoring the stop sign, turned left at a crossroads ahead of me, away from town. I rolled up to the T-intersection trying to calm down. My hands were tingling and starting to go numb. A revelation dawned as I looked at the fork ahead of me: I was in trouble. There was no more denying my marriage was over. My heart had thrown a rod and smoke was pouring out of my life. There was a choice to make. I could turn right, go home, and abandon the chase, or turn left and continue chasing after—what?

Wiping my nose on my sleeve, I turned right.

I went straight to my friends' home—a married couple I trusted and felt safe with. As soon as Jimmy opened the door and saw my face, he knew something terrible had happened. I cried in his arms as his wife, Marsha, prayed over me and fixed me a cup of hot tea. They offered to let me spend the night in their spare room, and I accepted. I couldn't be alone.

That night a piece of my heart died. As my dear friends consoled me, reality set in. My life was going to change, and the only way to survive this was to run to Jesus. He could rescue me. He could help me release my bitterness, heal my heart, help me to forgive, and restore my hope for a future. I wasn't even thinking about the kids. I was just trying to breathe.

MORE ON BIBLICAL FORGIVENESS

Seventy Times Seven

My neighbor, Tyrell, was twenty-six when his girlfriend got pregnant. Although he loved her very much, his affection wasn't reciprocated, and she refused his proposal. By the time their little girl Jasmine was three, they split—never married.

"I thought it was only a temporary separation, so I didn't fight for any rights. I was certain we'd reconcile," explains Tyrell. "When she started dating Jeff and then married him, it really bothered me. One day I was talking to my daughter on the phone and she started giggling. I asked her what was so funny. She said, 'Mr. Jeff's tickling me.' I was like, 'What?' It's painful to know some other guy is touching your daughter and making her laugh. There are sacred things in a little girl's relationship that should be reserved for only a daddy. I felt like he was interfering with our conversation to annoy me, flaunting his position. I was furious."

Tyrell dealt with his hurt in a mature manner, refusing to resort to retribution. Not everyone has good judgment. Whether it's picking up the kids late just to annoy the mother or worse, bringing a hot new girlfriend along—you're going to be tempted to be a jerk.

Don't.

Brock is another single father. His indulgence wasn't revenge—it was financial restitution. He worked at a lawyer's office and had powerful friends. With the divorce, Brock received custody of their twins and all the furniture. The judge ordered the tired old house to Sandra. When Sandra sold all the items to pay her bills, Brock sued her for violating the divorce decree because she was unable to surrender his furniture. The court fees cost him more than the furniture, but he felt justice had to be served. It didn't stop there.

Brock liked to dress his kids well. He bought the boys high-end clothing. Yet each time they visited Mom, they came back instead with worn-out clothes that were stained and too small. After several attempts to retrieve the clothes, Brock decided he needed more child support from his ex-wife. Another court date was set.

Last I heard from Brock, he was seeking monetary restitution for emotional distress and counseling. The twins must be in their teens now. I dare speculate what his sons are learning about forgiveness from good ol' dad.

Forgiveness toward a spouse who leaves you is a different journey for each individual. Some find it takes only months, others need decades. For me, it was an ongoing process. Just when I would work through one offense with my ex-wife, another incident would pop up, and I'd have to process that with the Lord until I came to peace with it. Incidents that affected my children were harder to forgive. I'm sure my ex felt the same about me.

Please don't hear something I'm not saying. There are times when you need to protect yourself to avoid being taken advantage of. Every situation is different. I'm just saying, ask for counsel and advice from others before deciding on your own what constitutes a defense strategy versus overlooking and forgiving. Choose your battles.

Dirty Laundry

While serving as theater arts director at my church, I also worked as a claims processor for a health insurance company. This particular day, I had been at the office about two hours when my ex-spouse walked in with both my children and headed straight for my desk. Normally I'd be thrilled to have the kids come see me at work. But I could see that too-familiar look on their mother's face that warned this was not a cordial visit.

My daughter and son greeted me with hugs and smiles, which quickly dropped when their mother began a verbal assault upon me. Taking the kids on my lap, I responded calmly, but this only escalated her anger.

I tried to remind her that this was not an appropriate place for a heated conversation, nor should the kids hear it.

I asked, "Shouldn't they be in school? Why did you bring—"

She continued, undeterred as my children stared blankly at the wall—no doubt confused how such an exciting visit to Daddy's office had somehow gone bad.

MAYO CLINIC'S BENEFITS OF FORGIVENESS

Lower blood pressure.
Risk of alcohol and substance abuse lowered.
Healthier relationships.
Decrease in depression symptoms.
Increased spiritual and psychological well-being.
Less anxiety, stress, and hostility.[1]

Embarrassed for her and knowing my coworkers were unable to concentrate, I walked to the door and called for security, asking them to escort my children and their mother out of the office. Before they could get there, she gathered our children and was leaving.

"Come on, kids, your father is kicking us out of the building."

As the door closed behind them, I heard one of my kids ask, "Why is Daddy making us leave?"

My heart squeezed with regret. How soon would I be able to explain the truth to them, and would they even understand?

I apologized to my coworkers for the disruption and sheepishly returned to my desk. My boss gave me a disapproving look as if I had invited the confrontation.

Because it involved my children, it took a long time to forgive their mother for that obviously planned attack—but I finally did. However, I learned I needed some better restrictions in place if I were to keep my job.

Boundaries

In the devotional poetry book, *Somewhere in the Journey*,[2] I have an entry titled "The Secret Judge." This talks about a friend who developed some very unrealistic opinions of me, attacking my character behind my back. I felt misunderstood and hurt. It was hard to forgive him and choose not to let this person steal my joy. Eventually we reconciled, but our relationship was never the same. Now I am cordial but keep our conversations brief and shallow. Not because I haven't forgiven this man, but because I've set up healthy boundaries to protect my family and myself from future attacks. This shouldn't be the norm, but when someone shows a track record of cycling hurt, don't be victimized. It's acceptable to install air bags in that relationship in order to shield us from being battered again. That's not a lack of forgiveness; it's wisdom.

Not only must we be diligent to chase down and kill bitterness, we also have to examine our own actions. Jesus tells us in Matthew 7 to first remove and repent of our own sinful actions and attitudes before trying to show others where they have screwed up.

This can be especially difficult if your former spouse is living an immoral lifestyle and your child is asking you about it. There's a temptation to turn the conversation into a lesson on the depravity of mankind, but don't. Refer them back to their mother for an answer. It's not for you to respond to your child; your ex-spouse needs to wrestle with answering that question herself.

Forgiving others increases our ability to hear from God more clearly. When we choose forgiveness, the Lord often instills a sense of peace and closure. It can be difficult, but when I choose forgiveness, I can feel his pleasure blanketing me, and my identity in Christ is strengthened. In the next chapter, we'll talk more about understanding our true identity and how it affects our fathering.

CHECKING YOUR GAUGES ———————————————————

It's important to know yourself well. How do you react to stress?

How can you better prepare yourself to respond to potentially stressful events?

Although we can't always protect our kids from everything in life, what are some ways you can prevent your children from seeing or hearing things above their comprehension level?

Do you need to ask forgiveness from someone you've sinned against? In what ways are you tempted to seek revenge or restitution? Who do you need to forgive?

STUDYING THE MAP

"Then Peter came to Jesus and asked, 'Lord how many times shall I forgive my brother or sister who sins against me? Up to seven times?' Jesus answered, 'I tell you, not seven times, but seventy-seven times."
Matthew 18:21–22 (NIV)

REROUTING

Read Matthew 5:11 and make it personal by adding your name. Write down the names of people who have offended or hurt you. Determine in your mind to forgive them and then begin praying for those people. Study Matthew 5:38–48 and meditate on what that means for you, practically.

REFUELING

Lord, I know it's impossible for me to predict every possible scenario that could happen to me or my children, so help me to respond well when difficult things occur. Give me a heart that runs to you in times of hurt or distress. Give me the emotional maturity to walk my children through difficult questions when they arise. Most of all, help me learn the healing art of forgiveness. Amen.

CHAPTER 5

Getting Some Bodywork Done
(God the Healer)

"Uh-oh, better call Maaco."

A divorce is much like a ten-car pileup. It affects not just two drivers but a whole slew of perimeter vehicles that get caught in the chaos. Not even innocent bystanders come out unscathed.

So you might feel totaled, like a pile of scrap metal. Take heart; you're not beyond some bodywork and a little loving care. In the right hands you could come out in better shape than before the crash.

Usually, the first thing you see when you climb out of the car is the damage. You know you're OK, but as steam pours from your radiator you hear a *ka-ching* in your head as you survey the needed repairs. With a divorce, it's a sinking feeling called *dread*.

During the months following my divorce I felt a knot in the pit of my stomach. Much like a car wreck, an overwhelming sense of hopelessness crumpled my mind.

I didn't know it at the time, but the reason I felt this way was that I had put my confidence in what I had acquired, not who I was in Christ. I thought my identity was in the things I had attained, and they were slipping away from me—my wife, my kids, my house, my cars—all of it.

Market Value

Looking at my life as if it were a listing on the Kelley Blue Book website was a mistake. When I entered all my features into the fields and clicked on the "appraisal" button, I didn't like the amount it calculated. My self-worth was way below the world's market price. This stung.

As I embraced the world's mentality, my actions followed suit. Desperate, I attempted to prove to the universe that I was an excellent father, a great employee, and a successful and desirable man. But it was all in

STEPS TOWARD EMOTIONAL RECOVERY

- Be honest with yourself, even if the truth hurts.
- Seek professional biblical counseling.
- Set healthy boundaries.
- Maintain positive relationships.
- Soak in God's presence and his Word.
- Forgive.
- Avoid those wrist-slitting country music songs you keep gravitating toward.

vain because I really didn't believe it. After all, how could I argue with the calculations from the internal appraisal I kept pondering?

In my feeble attempts to appear respectable, the opposite began to happen. I needed to pay the mortgage on the house my wife was living in, while paying rent on my own apartment. As a result, I lost my car to the repo man, got fired from my job, and had to move to a seedy part of town in order to afford the rent. Worst of all, the kids didn't enjoy living with me during this season.

My transmission was slowly slipping as I went down the road to becoming one of those clueless fathers you often see in films. I could feel failure encroaching upon my dignity like an infection. Obviously, I lacked understanding for why I'm placed on this earth. In all my years of living for the Lord I somehow missed that it was about him and not my own happiness or success.

It was in the midst of this when I called out to the Lord for help. I was tired of my journey. All my life had been an uphill climb to accomplish little more than a few trophies that had been wiped out. Life was vanity, nothing but striving for petty ghost treasures.

God's Day Spa

I remember lying on my bare, secondhand mattress, asking God with tears in my throat, "Is this all there is to this Christian life—just serving you until I'm dead? Is that all I get for my faithfulness all these years—a life of servitude with nothing to show for it?"

Now I won't go into a long biblical explanation about the skewed thinking I adopted in that moment of self-pity. There is a lot wrong with that whole mind-set. What I will say is that the next week in church the Lord overlooked all those offensive questions, bent down from heaven, and replied to me.

You might say I had a total makeover. It was an experience with the Almighty that has forever changed my relationship with him. I can only describe it as a tangible touch from God. I was lost in worship when a tingle washed over my body much like a low electrical current. It was followed by what felt like warm thick oil being poured over me. Although the Holy Spirit abides in us as Christians from the start of our conversion, much like an old car—we tend to leak. I had been leaking the oil of the Holy Spirit for a long time and he was filling me up again. It was gloriously healing.

Tears flowed down my face, and I looked around—nobody was staring at me. That was good. Nobody had noticed anything strange. I closed my eyes and continued to worship, reveling in this holy moment enveloping me.

I was a broken man. Whatever God was doing, I wanted to respond. I whispered to the Lord, "I'm not sure you really love me, God. Look at my life. You didn't stop any of this. I must be a rotten husband for my wife to leave me for another man. And you let it happen, Father. Why is my life such a joke? I'm a joke. What have I done that you would abandon me?"

Right about then I felt hot breath against my ear. Someone had walked up to me and was whispering the kindest words: "I'm your only true hope. I love you. I like you. You're my son, and you bring me great joy."

My eyes flew open, and I turned to look at—nothing. There was no human nearby, but I had definitely felt breath on my ear and the rich resonant depth of a kind, male voice.

WHAT IS SPIRITUAL BREATHING?

I broke into sobs. I knew who it was, and the fact that he would bend down and take the time to speak to me was overwhelming. I knew whatever measly relationship I was trying to have with my Heavenly Father before then was a joke. This God of mine wanted a full-on friendship, and I knew I wouldn't survive without it.

Additionally I saw how chaotic my life was because I had placed idols on the throne of my heart rather than allowing God to sit there. I repented, asking Christ to take his rightful place on that throne. Then I prayed for the Holy Spirit to rearrange my priorities, placing them under the control of the Father instead of me. The late Bill Bright, founder of Cru, calls this "spiritual breathing." Rightly so, because I exhaled my sin and inhaled the Spirit of God.

That evening the relationship between us became more than King and loyal subject. We became more than just a Master and slave, more than Father and child. I already knew how to relate to him in those arenas.

That night, I understood that the Master of the Universe desired to reveal himself as my friend and defender.

The feeling of warm oil continued over and through me. I felt my heart being healed of the hurt and rejection. Not just the emasculating wounds from the divorce and all the self-blame, but I felt every hurt from every childhood wound, every harsh word or action that had embedded itself into my psyche, all being healed by the hands of the One who loved me more than anyone ever could.

I wanted to be a rock for my kids, so they could feel some sense of stability. But what I really needed to do was teach them to make Christ their Rock. I certainly couldn't teach this without first believing it myself.

Up until this moment, I felt like God's problem child. That he loved me only because he had to. There was no way I could model the truth to my kids if I didn't believe it myself. So when my true identity in Christ was finally revealed to me, I understood what it meant to be chosen, accepted, adopted, bought with a price, part of his family, complete in Christ.

Now I'm not saying everyone will experience something like I did. Perhaps I just needed a little extra help in understanding truth. Most times, it's by simply studying the Bible and staying plugged into a local church that we begin to fully understand God's great love. The Word of God helps lift focus off ourselves and toward Jesus. Immersing ourselves in Scripture keeps us from believing ridiculous lies.

Now let me make it clear, although this supernatural experience was awesome, I still spent months studying Scripture passages and soaking in sermons or books to help reprogram my brain. The roots of those lies went deep into my heart and wouldn't disappear overnight. But as my security in Christ grew, I was able to model this for my kids.

As followers of Jesus, as sons of God, we don't need to calculate our worth by the world's standards. When we understand our significance comes from who we are in Christ, it defeats thoughts of failure. Reading 2 Timothy 1:7 we have to ask ourselves, why should we fear trials and tribulations when he has not given us a fearful disposition? These trials are perfecting us into mighty men of valor. His heart is toward us with loving kindness and compassion (Lam. 3:21–23). So why should we feel alone, confused, or even cursed? If we do, he wants to whisper in our ears, "I love you. I revel over you, favored one."

Take heart, friend. He likes us—a lot! Understanding this yourself will transfer that same sense of acceptance and stability to your child.

CHECKING YOUR GAUGES ───────────────────────────────

When do you feel most inadequate as a father?

How do you usually react to those feelings?

When is it hardest to embrace the fact that the Father actually revels over you and is proud of you?

STUDYING THE MAP

> *"The LORD your God is with you, the Mighty Warrior who saves. He will take great delight in you; in his love he will no longer rebuke you, but will rejoice over you with singing." Zephaniah 3:17 (NIV)*

REROUTING

Ask the Lord to show you how much he loves and values you. Ask a friend to help you remember occasions in your life where God has shown himself particularly active in running to help you in times of need or has showered his favor upon you.

Make two columns on a sheet of paper. In one column, list the last five years. In the other column, write one thing God did for you in each corresponding year. Cut them apart and hang them around the house to remind yourself of his favor on you over the years.

REFUELING

> *Father, I need you desperately in my life. I repent of any priorities I've allowed to take your place. Remind me to place my worth in you and your promises. Help me reject the lie that I'm defined by what my life looks like on the outside. You not only love me, you like me, and you see me with rose-colored glasses. When I do mess up, remind me of my right standing and new identity in Christ. Amen.*

CHAPTER 6

Regular Tune-Ups, Part 1
(Social/Mental/Spiritual Health)

"The timing's a little off but she still runs great."

Traveling by plane doesn't seem complicated these days. However, when the flight attendant begins giving instructions about crisis procedures, you realize things are very different from earthbound travel—the drop-down mask in particular. No other form of public transportation requires oxygen in case of an emergency. Clearly, you are to take care of yourself first, before attempting to care for any children. It makes sense. How can you help anyone else if you aren't getting oxygen to your brain? You can't think straight or formulate sensible decisions when you're on the verge of passing out. It's the same with parenting alone. How often I have seen single parents attempt to care for their children when they themselves are obviously in need of some quiet time, a little community, or counseling.

It was springtime. Suddenly single again, I was losing weight. I wasn't trying to get slimmer to find a woman; I was just forgetting to eat. There was a lot of stress in my life and some things were neglected in order to cope. I was only able to keep a few essential things in focus—my kids' welfare, my job, and the search for basic shelter. My hygiene was cut back to a shower and brushing my teeth. I often forgot to shave or put on deodorant. I didn't always feel the need to get dressed on the weekends either. It took all I had to juggle the basics. I ate to stay alive. A bean burrito and a cup of water at the drive-thru fueled my body. My car interior became my second apartment. Life was dismal.

Before long, it was evident I was becoming weird. Here's my philosophy about us men: if we don't maintain some type of community with others, we regress. I needed to stabilize my social, mental, spiritual, emotional, and physical lives. To better understand, let's explore those areas.

Social Health

Juan lived alone and was becoming a bit of a hermit. One day he and I were waiting for dessert at a coffee shop when he began clipping his fingernails. I watched him for a moment with horrible visions of one of those clippings accidentally flying into someone's latté. It took about two fingernails for me to muster the gumption and ask him to stop.

MALE PERFORMANCE ISSUES

No, this isn't a tip on sexual stamina, but it got your attention, didn't it?

Some men desire to perform like a hero when it comes to just about anything, including child support. This can get guys into trouble if your former spouse is never satisfied monetarily. Embarrassing gossip can pressure even the best of providers to defend their reputation unnecessarily.

Know your limits and understand some people will never have enough money. However, if the issue is valid, at the request of your ex the courts will revisit the amount and increase your financial responsibility accordingly.

"Sorry, I guess public grooming isn't exactly vogue." He laughed, looking out the window. "I think I've been an island for too long."

We had a good laugh at the truth. We men are funny—some of us can become feral without others in our lives. After all, community teaches us important life skills. Perhaps God saw Adam's need for community when he created Eve. When I find myself talking to and naming my volleyball Wilson, it's probably a good idea for me to strategically seek the company of others, even if I don't want to. Community helps me stay in touch with reality—like oxygen for my brain. Being in the company of others was a precious place for stabilizing myself and thinking clearly as I rebuilt my life.

There's something to be said about relatives too. Give them a chance to minister to you. Although many of my family didn't always live nearby, their prayers were felt. When I experienced low moments I'd find a card or letter in the mail from my father, encouraging me to press on.

The Lord used my singleness to reconnect me to my brothers and their families too. My eldest brother, Ron, sent me e-mails from time to time reminding me to rely on the Holy Spirit for strength and power. My brother Wayne visited me soon after my separation. During those single-again years, he was instrumental in helping me think through issues logically, rather than through the emotional lens that often clouded my decisions. Another brother, Fred, reassured me as he sat on the floor of my living room. I had no furniture, but inside my sad little 400-square foot apartment on the wrong side of town, he looked at me with empathy and said just one hope-giving sentence, "It won't always be this way."

He was right. With the Lord's help I overcame that season and I'm better for it.

Mental Health

It was Saturday morning and my weekend without the kids. I got up, ate a cold toaster pastry with a cup of coffee, and then flopped across the bed. I woke up again at two in the afternoon, showered, and turned on the television.

After a few hours of sitcom reruns, I stared out my kitchen window to the parking lot below. It was empty except for my vehicle. Everyone else had a life. Two little boys I had never seen before rode into the parking lot on bicycles. They circled my automobile a few times, and then one of them reached down, grabbed a small stone from the ground, and rode closer to my car. In an instant he reached out and carved a big line along the whole side of the vehicle, scratching the paint as he pedaled. A normally healthy car owner would have run down the stairs and outside to catch them. I didn't even flinch. They rode away, and I just sighed and walked back to the couch.

By dinnertime, still in my robe, I ate some noodles with butter, wondering if antidepressants should be on the menu. Reading the newspaper, I fell asleep by nine.

Sunday was a repeat.

A friend of mine suggested I try visiting a Christian counselor on the weekends when I didn't have the kids. That was one of the best pieces of advice I got. Using the Word of God, my counselor encouraged and coached me back to a healthier place. Someone speaking truth into my life and praying with me was exactly what I needed. Before long, I was filling my empty weekends helping a city police chaplain. For me, serving others helped restore a sense of worth and purpose. When not at work, I strategically replaced any free time by volunteering for the police department. I made sure to engage my mind outwardly, rather than allowing it to wander or silently entertain a myriad of unhealthy thoughts about my wife and her new lover.

Spiritual Health

Prayer and Bible reading can be life-giving practices during times of stress and adjustment. Sadly, because I'm prone to independence, I struggle with this even today. I have to be proactive and schedule time seeking God or else I stray back into the sin of self-sufficiency. But talking to God is not formal. I love how 1 Peter 5:7 reminds me how he craves to hear our hearts, our dreams, our disappointments. I remember times when all I could do was stare at the fire escape outside my window and whisper, "God, help me." Nonetheless, it was a prayer, and he was listening—waiting for it.

If all you can read is a few sentences of God's Word each day, then at least do that. If you have to, listen to an audio version as you fall sleep. In whatever way you can absorb his life-giving Holy Scripture into your head, get it in there. Isaiah 26:3 says, "You will guard him *and* keep him in perfect *and* constant peace whose mind [both its inclination and its character] is stayed on You, because he commits himself to You, leans on You, *and* hopes confidently in You" (AMP).

So what about church? For some single dads, going to church is not as enjoyable as it used to be. Sitting alone in the same pew that used to hold your entire family can be difficult. Perhaps you have an ex who still attends, and you're both fighting over who gets custody of the church.

FIVE WAYS TO MINISTER TO SINGLE DADS

Aaron was extremely charming, but he didn't know it. He discovered married couples didn't know quite how to interact with him now that he was suddenly single. He said at times he felt like dead wood on pruning day. Most of the time it was just his own insecurities, but Aaron sensed couples viewed him as a threat—a freewheeling bachelor on the hunt. This wasn't true, but he couldn't really address the issue comfortably with his married friends without appearing paranoid.

I noticed he started to avoid coming to church. I knew it was critical he find a solution and turn toward (not away from) believers who could encourage, challenge, and spur him on in love. Aaron knew this but didn't feel at home there anymore. Eventually he moved away and found a new body of believers—that was OK. The point is, he didn't stop meeting with believers. He understood the urgency of surrounding himself with a community of Christ followers.

CHECKING YOUR GAUGES

What are some ways you can ensure community is a priority in your life?

How have you allowed the local church to be a safe harbor?

STUDYING THE MAP

"A calm and undisturbed mind and heart are the life and health of the body, but envy, jealousy, and wrath are like rottenness of the bones." Proverbs 14:30 (AMP)

REROUTING ————————————————————————

Create a quiet-time schedule if you don't have one already. Perhaps you need to make an appointment with a counselor or something simpler, like just getting to bed earlier.

REFUELING ————————————————————————

Dear Father, I can't do this alone. You have to help me, because anything I do without you is basically trash. Surround me with godly friends and help me be more intentional in nurturing new relationships. Heal every part of me and let it overflow toward my children. Amen.

CHAPTER 7

Regular Tune-Ups, Part 2
(Emotional/Physical Health)

"I'm not crying; I just have something in my eye."

Dustin's wife passed away more than two years ago, but he was still exhausted with grief. "I'm operating on a deficit. I want to be more consistent when I discipline the boys, but I just can't find the energy. There's nothing left in me to follow through."

My heart went out to Dustin. He was emotionally spent. Being so drained pulls down our physical stamina as well. In the last chapter we discussed social, mental, and spiritual health. Let's continue with some other areas that may need attention.

Emotional Health

Pastor Thomas gently smiled at me. "When did you last cry? I mean real tears."

I shrugged. The separation was twelve months behind me. I wasn't really upset about the breakup anymore. I had accepted it months ago. It was more about the kids now. I was angry they would not have the childhood I'd dreamed they would have.

If I allowed myself to grieve, that would be embracing the irreversible. If I stayed mad, I could maybe change things—force my ex to correct some wrongs that impacted my children.

"Your family situation is what it is, Tez. Staying mad won't fix Sharaya's

"Be man enough to be hurt."
—Mike Klumpp[1]

and Caleb's future. Before our next session I want you to go somewhere private, put your face on the floor, and pour your heart out to Jesus. I mean just bust your guts mourning if you need to. Because turning it into anger, Tez, just makes you end up sinning in some way or another."

Pastor Thomas was right. My anger wouldn't change things for my kids, at least not for the better. Later that night I released my resentment and began grieving over my kids' losses—things they would never know they lost.

I grabbed a roll of toilet paper—because it's manlier than a box of tissues, right? I began repenting to the Lord, then mourning over my children.

I thought about all the norms that would never be. The family vacations without a mom, the holidays without a dad, the everyday conversations that occur over dinner or while driving to school. The little teaching opportunities while taking walks or working in the yard. Conversations about manners, finances, romance, and heaven. I knew these moments would still happen, but not in the fashion I had hoped. One parent would often be missing from these discussions—causing unbalanced experiences and lessons.

Like me, there could be a time when you need to let a dream die. It's the dream of a different life for your child. You might even observe that the two-household family may not be as big a deal to your child as you thought it would be. If your child is young enough, it may hardly ruffle their feathers. For them, life will be what it will be.

For me, this dream had been more about my needs than theirs. Maybe that's why I was so furious. It had become all about me, and I was annoyed because I wasn't getting what I wanted. Nobody around me seemed to want what I wanted.

My selfishness now revealed, I began to weep—slowly at first, then like a levy in a hurricane. Thirty minutes later, I found myself on the floor of my bedroom earnestly petitioning God—mediating on my children's behalf. At one point I remember taking their photos off the dresser and waving them in the air—lifting their names to the Father, in prayer. I interceded for them so passionately I thought my neck

veins would pop. When I was too exhausted to go on, I took a deep breath for closure, went to the mirror, and laughed at myself. My face was as puffy as a Botox junkie, but my burden suddenly felt a lot lighter.

Physical Health

Seven years later I found myself working the night shift and sharing a house with a good friend, Derek. My son, Caleb (now eleven years old), was also living with me full-time. It was like a godly version of the sitcom *Two and a Half Men*. On school days, Derek would wake up Caleb as he left for work. My son got ready for school with no adult supervision. I hated this and beat myself up for it daily. I would arrive home just as he was walking out to meet the school bus. Exhausted, and intoxicated with guilt, I'd kiss him good-bye and sleep until he returned. Then I'd make dinner, help Caleb with homework, watch a little television with him, tuck him into bed, and leave for work.

Thankfully Derek had an incredible servant's heart. He was willing to forfeit any social life he might rather have, in order to stay at home all evening with my son. Together with the help of our church, we provided Caleb with the male companionship he needed during this crucial time in his life. With Caleb's mother three states away, many of the women at church doted on him. Caleb seemed to especially love that. It wasn't the best situation, but it's all I could offer as a single parent.

Sometimes I wondered, *What am I thinking?* My overall health wasn't responding well to this nocturnal lifestyle. Sure the graveyard shift offered better pay than more traditional hours, but at what cost? I didn't have any energy to care for my son. I was gaining weight, not exercising, and very lethargic. Was I forfeiting my health by working nights? Derek had a fantastic heart. He was a single guy with a lot more energy to entertain my son, but he was not a dad. He had no parenting experience. I was so tired I didn't care. Caleb never complained, but I knew I was physically becoming less and less able to care for him like I should. I relied heavily on my small group and the singles ministry to help me raise my boy. My neediness doubled when my daughter visited.

I'm no doctor and certainly not a nutritionist. But there are basics that everyone knows. Here are a few, in no particular order:

- Get at least six to eight hours of uninterrupted sleep
- Choose healthier foods (more plants—less starch/sugars/fat)
- Drink eight tall glasses of water a day
- Do cardio exercise at least twenty minutes a day
- Read books more than you watch TV/movies
- Invest time in developing yourself (occupationally and personally)
- Remove unhealthy stressors and allow yourself to laugh more
- Get away from your mobile device for a couple hours a day
- Do something you enjoy on your days off
- Help others
- Follow Christ with all your heart, mind, body, and soul

There's no way I can care properly for my children if I don't first care for myself. So I slowly began cooking healthier meals and exercising more. I chose fewer movies and more active choices with the singles group at church—bringing Caleb along.

I adjusted my resting habits too. Because sleep begets sleep, I found that if I slept too much it just made me drowsier. I made sure to limit myself to sleeping no more than eight hours. With a little B12 and more sunlight I felt changes taking place. I wasn't as dull, and my conversations with others became sharper.

My fathering followed suit. Caleb and I spent more time together, and I found I didn't need to depend so much on others. Before long I was back on my game.

CHECKING YOUR GAUGES ————————————————————————

Grieving isn't a one-time event; it comes in waves. How have you allowed
    yourself to grieve lately?

What unhealthy practices do you engage in that may negatively affect
    your children?

What part of yourself do you feel most needs improvement? What game
    plan do you have to ensure healthy change?

STUDYING THE MAP ————————————————————————
    *"No discipline seems pleasant at the time, but painful. Later on,
    however, it produces a harvest of righteousness and peace for those
    who have been trained by it." Hebrews 12:11 (NIV)*

REROUTING ————————————————————————
    Fill up your free time with something productive. Consider volunteer-
ing somewhere that's fun and energizes you. Christian parachurch orga-
nizations or a local church are just two great places to start.

REFUELING ————————————————————————
    *Lord, I desperately need you to keep me emotionally and physically
    healthy so I can be a better dad. Please give me the strength to recover
    my emotional well-being and steward well this body you gave me.
    Amen.*

CHAPTER 8

Prepping the Motor Home
(Creating a New Space)

"Dude, you gotta check out my awesome man cave."

I grew up camping a few times a year. My father was a prominent leader for Royal Rangers, a Christian boys' club. As sons of a Regional Commander, my brothers and I were expected to earn all our badges and be excellent campers. Celebrity survivalist Bear Grylls would be proud of me because I can probably live for days in the wilderness on grubs and dew. That doesn't mean I enjoy it. In fact, as a teen, I vowed never again to sleep on a cold tent floor or smell like campfire smoke. I appreciate hotels with amenities. Although I know a hotel is just an illusion of a real home, I still appreciate the effort. When I travel, I like to retain a small sense of stability and comfort—I can't get that from a lean-to in the woods.

Yet, I still love adventure. I once had the opportunity to drive my family across America in a midsized recreational vehicle. We rented an RV and trekked across America.

Just so we're clear, an RV is *not* camping, so I was OK with this.

One thing that makes a motor home adventure more enjoyable is the effort the manufacturer takes to make the RV a bit more like a home. You get to enjoy the comfort of beds, a shower, closets—even curtains.

My family and I fashioned treasured memories as we took our time stopping at many of the tasteless, Americana roadside attractions. In forty days we made our way from California to Florida. What made the trip more pleasant were the little things we did to help us feel at home—bringing a favorite pillow, a family photo, or just a souvenir fridge magnet. The trip was a success, but had we neglected to bring a few reminders from home, we might have quickly tired of life on the road. Just a few years earlier I had learned the hard way to make things homier.

GET A MENTOR

The male bowerbirds of Australia construct elaborately decorated nests, or bowers, to attract females. Different local populations of bowerbirds build nests that exhibit different decorative styles. Building styles are culturally acquired, rather than genetically transmitted. Some say young male bowerbirds are inept at bower-building and spend years watching their elders before becoming accomplished in the local bower style.[1]

The Infamous Dog Bed

It was during the first weeks of my divorce when I realized I was neglecting the importance of a welcoming environment for my kids. I made sure my daughter, Sharaya, had a bed, but for my son I made the mistake of being a little cheap by purchasing a dog bed. Yes, you read that right—a dog bed! You know, the large round kind you buy for a Labrador retriever or German shepherd.

I'm such an idiot.

The pooch cushion was new, clean, and comfortable. Caleb was young enough to enjoy the idea rather than be disgusted. He would lie down on it, wrap it over himself like a giant taco shell, and giggle himself to sleep. He never complained, but when I tucked him in and saw him on the ground sleeping in a canine cot, I knew it was an absurd idea. I was getting weird, and my kids were paying the price. I quickly got a real bed for Caleb. Today, that dog mat is probably under a bridge somewhere, making some homeless guy very happy.

Becoming Mrs. Doubtfire

Men, your new accommodations shouldn't feel temporary. In the midst of chaos, we need to make life for our kids as normal and homey as possible. If we're the noncustodial parent, we must create the illusion of something more permanent so our kids don't feel they are camping out for the weekend in our man cave. At the very least, we should make it a motor home experience, if not something better. Allowing our kids to live out of a piece of luggage every other weekend probably shouldn't be a long-term option. Purchase an affordable bed and dresser from a yard sale, if you can. It might help to have a few extra sets of clothes for them at your house, which *stay* at your house. Give your child a shelf in the bathroom they can call their own. Maybe have some kid-friendly food in the freezer. Nothing says, "This isn't your home, kid," louder than a fridge that only contains moldy cheese and a bottle of beer.

We've all seen movies where the newly single dad thinks this is his second chance at being a swinging bachelor. Hollywood is notorious for portraying us as dim-witted losers with pizza boxes on the bed and unwashed clothes in the bathtub. Don't laugh; filmmakers got that idea from somewhere.

If your child lives with you full-time, then raise the bar even more. They need to feel safe. That feeling is detected by the child through all five senses. Take a moment to use your own sensory skills to get a feel for what message you're sending. Have you left potentially dangerous tools on the living room floor? Does the house smell like a garage? When you speak, are the acoustics echoed for lack of fabric in the house? Do you feel grit when you walk around barefoot? Do all your recipes taste like Tabasco? If you answered "Yes" to any of these questions, your environment doesn't send a message of safety. Your kids may not be able to pinpoint where it's coming from, but they won't enjoy life at Dad's house.

Making your place a warm and inviting environment is all part of parenting. Now I'm not saying we need to feminize our role by trying to be both a father and a mother. The male role is already enough at risk. What I mean is, we should try to decorate our homes with maturity and good taste. For a season, I utilized a southwestern décor with clay pots and cactuses. With that in mind I was able to create a welcoming environment that was still manly.

Don't get crazy though. For instance, if you decide on animal prints, you don't want your home to look like Africa threw up all over your house. Remember less is more. Learn to accent, not overwhelm. If you need to, ask a female relative to offer ideas on transforming your pad into a masculine, yet family-friendly place. Put away your college relics, like that lampshade of beer cans, and buy a man candle—yes, they exist. I found one that was grey and smelled like cedar. Anyway, our kids need us to be the dad, not a fun single uncle. When you can replace your 007 poster with a framed portrait of Grandma, your kids will experience an underlying sense of being home when they are with you—whether for a weekend, a summer, or full-time.

I guess what I'm saying is, man-up and decorate!

A SAFE HARBOR

Every time I get into the car I make sure everyone is buckled. In fact our family has a fun, meaningless code word. I have no idea why we chose it, but once we're buckled up, we shout out "Aloha!" Until I hear each person say it, I don't drive away.

Safety is just as important as we journey through our new lives as single fathers. Whether it's baby-proofing your house for your toddler, putting parental controls on the TV for your teens, or practicing a fire escape, make sure you think carefully through anything that could go wrong due to careless oversight. A safe home is a happy home.

CHECKING YOUR GAUGES ———————————————

How might your words or actions reinforce a sense of permanence rather than camping?

In what environment do your kids seem most relaxed?

How can you duplicate that environment to make your home more comfortable for them?

If you are not gifted in the area of home décor and aesthetics, what are
some ways you can hone those skills?

STUDYING THE MAP
> *"When I was a child, I spoke like a child, I thought like a child,
> I reasoned like a child. When I became a man, I gave up childish
> ways." 1 Corinthians 13:11*

REROUTING

Don't trust yourself. Ask a friend to look around your house and suggest what you can change to make it more inviting for your children. If
funds are an issue, check out garage sales or secondhand stores. In fact,
take the kids with you and include them in the process of finding their
furniture or accessories. This fosters a sense of ownership for them.

REFUELING
> *Lord, please teach me how I can improve the place where my family
> and I live. Father, make my domain a place of refuge for my chil-
> dren, especially during stressful changes. I ask that you cause them
> to look forward to coming home to Dad and that our times together
> would be relaxing and enjoyable. Let them feel your Holy Spirit in
> every corner of my house. In Jesus's name, amen.*

CHAPTER 9

The Drive-Thru
(Cooking Basics)

"What's a cutting board?"

"Are we having hot dogs again, Dad?" My son curled up his nose.

"Nope. We're having fried bologna." I smiled, pulling a pan from the cabinet.

My daughter shook her head and stared out the window with a look that said, "I hate being here."

I was very proud of myself actually. I had made a choice that week to try harder as a cook. Both kids were now living with me full-time. As the custodial parent, I needed to up my game. It was not an easy road, and my kids suffered through some weird meals.

Many of you guys will find cookbooks a useful remedy. I just needed meals with less math and more fun. My best friend says cooking is both a science and an art. There are times when you must obey the exact instructions or the meal refuses to turn out well. Sometimes there are scientific issues that must be calculated. For instance, baking the same cake in the mountains requires a slightly different recipe from baking that same cake in the lowlands. That's just science.

Yet cooking is also an art. Being a very creative guy, I dreaded trying to decipher recipes and cookbooks—still do. I hate instructions but love to prepare meals if I can make it a work of inspiration. I add a bit of this and a little of that and taste it. Drop in a pinch of something else and then sample it

again. Much like when I'm paint-
ing on a canvas, I stand back and
look at my creation, adding what I
think it needs to craft my own private masterpiece. Granted, much
like my artwork, my meals never
turn out the same way twice. I
don't mind; I appreciate variety.

KILL IT AND GRILL IT

Whether it's a rusted-out hiba-
chi filled with old charcoal or a
six-foot shiny propane mega-grill
with six side burners, there's
something impressive about a
guy who can serve up a meal
off the grill. Learn how and learn
now.

You need to decide for yourself
what side of cooking you prefer—the science or the art. In the end, you're
going to have to embrace that it's both, but you can enjoy the chore of
meal preparation a lot more once you decide how to look at it.

May I Take Your Order?

Grocery shopping was intimidating. Stores have so many flavor and
ingredient variations for each type of food. Should I buy no-brand or the
expensive foods? Would we taste the difference? On top of this, the aisles
were filled with everything from jumbo to miniature travel-sized rations.
Larger quantities were less expensive, yet single-serving portions alleviated food going bad before I could use it. Who could I call to help me
decide what to do? I dare not ask my ex-wife. So I would stand in one aisle
for thirty minutes, trying to figure out the best deal.

When I finally reached the frozen food section it was glorious. Much
like rolling up to the colorful menu at a fast-food joint, I was overwhelmed, but in a good way. So many choices and the pictures on the
boxes looked so delicious. Surely when cooked, each treat looked exactly
like the image on the box, right?

I usually left the store spending way too much for too few groceries. I
knew I needed help but being single I couldn't just ask any female to join
me shopping. Asking the wrong person could feel weird. I feared it may
look like a flirtation in disguise. It never crossed my mind to ask someone
safe like my sister-in-law or someone's grandmother to accompany me for
a few shopping lessons.

BUFFALO CHICK-WICH

1 sub roll, sliced
2 frozen chicken tenders
2 T. hot wing sauce
½ cup mozzarella cheese

Prepare chicken tenders according to package directions. While hot, toss in wing sauce and place on roll. Top with cheese and heat in 500 degree oven until edges are browned. Add blue cheese dressing for dipping (optional).

When it comes to meals, I can be somewhat lazy. It's much easier to whip out some toaster pastries than to make an omelet. Left on my own back then, meals for my kids gravitated toward frozen foods. The microwave oven provided easy, quick solutions. My pantry and refrigerator became a drive-thru window of sorts, filled with cheap, fast, unhealthy foods. Things like cereal, frozen burritos, frozen pizzas, corned beef hash, potato chips, soda, and ice cream. If I felt particularly domestic, I'd pull out a store-bought lasagna from the back of the freezer, chip the ice away, and nuke the red brick until it was room temperature. As my kids pushed the food around with forks and sighed, I would smile, clueless. Surely their blank stares into the plates confirmed I was indeed as awesome as I thought.

Honestly, I love eating—not cooking. But if Jesus could do it (John 21), I suppose I could try. I eventually learned how to make the chore rewarding and still fill my family's bellies.

I started with boxed macaroni and cheese, then I moved up to what I called Bachelor's Fettuccini, which was (don't laugh) just egg noodles, butter, sour cream, and Parmesan cheese. Again, I kept no recipes. I just added things until they tasted right. Either of these dishes could be upgraded by including ground beef and corn. Add a premade bagged garden salad, and I had a complete dinner in ten minutes. Bam!

Well OK, maybe it was pretty sorry, and definitely not attractive on a plate, but it was a step up from canned ravioli.

Then one day I finally discovered the wonderful magic of (insert angel choir here) the slow cooker!

Ah, the slow cooker; a single parent's dream. Fill it with food, slap on the lid, turn it on, and go to work. When you come home, dinner is served. Although that first day I returned and realized I had forgotten to plug it in. Lesson learned. I displayed a fake smile and said, "All right, kids, how about peanut butter and jelly?"

Would You Like Fries with That?

Let's talk about healthy sides for a moment. First off, let's clear this up—fries are not a side dish and you can't count those as a vegetable. Sorry.

If your darling little sweeties won't eat things like salads or other green foods, try something fun like ants on a log (raw celery sticks with peanut butter and raisins on top). I found if I could come up with a fun name for some new side dish I attempted, the kids will try just about any cuisine for fear of missing out on something awesome.

Guys, it's so easy to provide a couple sides that there's really no excuse for us these days. Buy some corn on the cob and boil it, or steam some firm broccoli in the microwave oven. Fresh produce rocks and makes you look awesome. I never could find a reason to buy a can of peas and carrots, but if that's your thing, go for it.

Can I Super-Size That for You?

Have you ever fed something to a stray dog? Not knowing when his next meal is coming, he scarfs it down without tasting it. He's in survival mode. When I was in college, I ate like a stray dog. I went for giant portions, and I didn't care how it looked. My motto was, "It all looks the same once it's chewed." So I would shovel it in, and that was the end of mealtime. Coming into fatherhood, I learned to slow down because my kids were modeling me. As I matured, I began caring about what I ingested and its effect on my health.

If, like me, you are anti-cookbook, a few basic rules of thumb might keep you from having to buy *Cooking for Newbies*. First of all, use color. If all the food on your plate is white or beige, it may not necessarily be a balanced meal. You might think it's sensible, but noodles, mashed potatoes, bread, and cauliflower is not only ugly—it's all carbs. If everything is green, it might be stupendously healthy, but you won't win any awards for presentation. Try to go for a dinner plate that includes a variety of hues from the color pallet. Often, this ensures a more balanced meal—but not always. Fruit Loops are colorful too, but use your head.

EASY NUTELLA COOKIES

1 cup Nutella
1 whole egg
1 cup flour
No sugar or butter

1. Plop spoonfuls onto an ungreased cookie sheet.
2. Bake for 6-8 min at 350 degrees.
3. Enjoy with a cold glass of milk. Yeah, baby!

Eventually you're going to find yourself needing to cook a full-blown meal. Either you'll invite a lady friend over for dinner, or maybe Thanksgiving dinner will be left up to you. Whatever the reason, you'll need to be prepared. Don't fret. I've got a few secrets to share with you.

If you don't mind cheating, local supermarkets usually offer a deli. There you can pick up a rotisserie chicken or even get a precooked turkey with all the fixings. Transfer those into your own dishes at home, and you're good to go.

Your kids, even if they are fairly young, can help you prepare a meal. Let them learn this life skill early on. Start them off with something easy, like tacos or an omelet. Think creatively. Leftovers can become unbelievably delicious ingredients for omelets. As your progeny assist you, be sure to speak clearly and explain exactly what you need done. Be very clear. Throwing out half sentences and rushed instructions will only produce a mess and set you back.

Another secret for making meals stretch is to add thinners or fillers—but carefully. Let's say your thirteen-year-old seems to be eating more than he did when he was five. Your best friend will become water or oatmeal or tofu. Just about any recipe will stretch if you add one of those ingredients. Experiment carefully with these; too much of any can ruin your meal also.

In addition, try not to poison your loved ones. Guys, I know some of you are leaving that used frying pan on the stove overnight and using it the next day for another meal. You know who you are; don't pretend I'm writing this for someone else. Let me tell you something. That's a gateway habit. Keep it up and before you know it, you'll be growing mushrooms on your shower floor and wearing your underwear inside out to avoid doing laundry. Stop it!

Cook everything properly. While raw beef and fish might make you sick, raw chicken and pork could kill you. Avoid cross-contamination when you cook by thoroughly washing your knives and cutting board with soap and hot water between different foods. If you're like me and many other guys, multitasking isn't a strength. If someone is talking to me while I'm cooking, he or she is pretty much gambling with their health. Staying focused in the kitchen keeps you and your kids out of the ER.

You might not be the next Chef Gordon Ramsay, but with a can opener, a pot, a frying pan, and a spatula, you just might turn into your kid's own famous chef.

I pray you don't have as hard of a time learning as I did. But making some effort is better than not trying at all. You and your kids deserve a healthy home-cooked meal. Believe in yourself.

One final thought.

Bacon.

CHECKING YOUR GAUGES

When was the last time you used the oven?

What is one meal you remember from your childhood that brings comforting thoughts?

Where do you find yourself on the list below? Ask your kids where they would place you.

_____ Starvin' Marvin (Never feeds the kids)

_____ Drive-Thru Dad (Eats from bags)

_____ Microwave Slave (Hates recipes)
_____ Spaghetti Eddie (Cooks simply. No frills)
_____ Captain Cook (Does pretty well in the kitchen)
_____ Celebrity Chef (Awesome, no skinny kids here)

STUDYING THE MAP

"Which of you fathers, if your son asks for a fish, will give him a snake instead? Or if he asks for an egg, will give him a scorpion? If you then, though you are evil, know how to give good gifts to your children, how much more will your Father in heaven give the Holy Spirit to those who ask him!" Luke 11:11–13 (NIV)

REROUTING

Buy a slow cooker this week. If you need to use frozen dinners, look for ones with vegetables. Replace those donuts with apples, and the sugary cereal with muesli. Fill that crisper drawer in the refrigerator with something green and leafy.

If you own a cookbook titled *100 Recipes for Spam*, get a different one. When eating out, choose family restaurants that offer hot, home-style meals.

REFUELING

Heavenly Father, gift me with creativity and wisdom when feeding my family. Help me become an experienced cook, and give me the know-how to prepare healthy balanced meals for the children you've entrusted into my care. In Jesus's name, amen.

PART 2

Changing Lanes

CHAPTER 10

Model Cars
(Avoiding Image Traps)

"I wouldn't be caught dead driving that."

"Ouch!" my friend Cody said as we bounced over a few potholes in the road.

The seller acknowledged, "Yeah, the shocks are ruined on this thing. I just haven't got around to replacing them. The heat isn't working either."

I had gone with Cody to check out this beautiful red Corvette he wanted to buy. It had been recently detailed and reupholstered inside. The engine sparkled, and it hummed beautifully.

However, this test drive we were now taking was revealing some underlying issues. Things were being neglected for the sake of appearances.

An automobile has more than just the obvious components that help it run properly. You also have underlying parts that must be attended to. If axles, radiators, exhaust system, electrical components, or other items are not up to par, they will eventually begin to show through. So it is with some of us dads.

In Genesis, God decided we need a helpmate. There's a reason for that. Raising kids with your wife as a team includes some accountability—mutual "maintenance required" reminders. It's usually as a new bachelor that we find ourselves overcompensating in order to overcome insecurities. It's not easy seeing our kids thrown into an unexpected lifestyle, so we often try to ease the transition in ways that aren't always flattering. Let's explore a few "Vehicle Dads."

The Jeep Dad

This dad loves to fill his children's lives with activity: amusement parks, movies, pool parties, and more. He makes sure his children get a toy with every kid's meal. He rarely disciplines his children. By the time he returns them to their mother, he's broke and the kids are tired, spoiled, and grumpy.

PRESENCE > PRESENTS

"Good fathers do three things: provide, nurture and guide. Yet too many men have warped ideas of what this means, it sets them up for feeling unworthy."
—Roland Warren of National Fatherhood Initiative[1]

The Jeep Dad is a good time, but he has no substance. He keeps himself and his family busy to avoid the hard work it takes to maintain depth of a relationship. He wins his children over with things. Although the kids love visiting Dad, equally they can't wait to get back home to the stability of Mom's house—the peace and quiet of normal life. When Jeep Dad has custodial rights and the kids are living with him full-time, he produces discontent children who consider everyday life mundane.

To avoid the Jeep Dad syndrome, try low-key, inexpensive activities like board games. Take walks together. Ask open-ended questions and wait for answers. Don't be afraid of silence. These relational-based activities help everyone slow down. They enrich everyone's experiences. When the kids are finally grown, it's the walks and talks they will remember, not the latest blockbuster movie.

The Hummer Dad

This guy is basically the Jeep Dad with money. His kids have clowns and ponies at their birthday parties. The Hummer Dad evolves from a Jeep Dad due to insecurities. He's become overly concerned about appearances, making sure he and his kids have all the latest electronic gadgets. Any inadequacies he might feel as a single parent are hidden behind the façade of success. He feels like more is better. His children not only get gaming systems, tablets, and smart phones with unlimited texting—they also benefit from Dad's toys. Much of this is bought in order to win the child's favor or to win the respect of other parents. Hummer Dad and his kids have adopted a consumer mind-set that says, "If it's for sale, we need to have it."

Perhaps this can be best explained from the viewpoint of a stepfather.

Jack married Anna, who had custody of a daughter from her previous marriage. Jack instantly bonded to little Mallory. He became the perfect bonus dad, making her his very own. Today, Mallory is a teen and their relationship is a shining example of love and respect for each other. You wouldn't guess Jack is not her biological father.

As it should be, Mallory's birth father, Roger, is still in the picture too. Roger and his daughter love one another very much and connect as often as they can. However, Roger suffers from H.D.S. (Hummer Dad syndrome).

Roger likes to give Mallory extravagant gifts when she visits him. Recently he rented a limo for Mallory and her girlfriends. He even took her to Italy one summer. Now I'm not about to pretend to guess why Roger is doing this. I have my suspicions. Had my own ex-wife ever remarried, I too might have resorted to such madness. The fear of losing my child's affections to a stepfather may have tempted me to try buying my daughter's love. Thankfully, I'll never know how low I might have stooped.

I've seen the effects this Hummer Dad, Roger, has on Jack and Anna. They can't provide that same level of luxury for Mallory that her biological father can. Each time Roger lavishes gifts on Mallory, Jack and Anna pay the price for it. They have to reprogram Mallory's expectations. The transition is frustrating for Jack and Anna, never fun for Mallory, and Roger isn't endearing himself to the two adults who could help him become a better father.

If your goal is to sabotage the efforts of your child's mother, then be Roger. But if you want to be known as a peacemaker, talk things over first. There's nothing wrong with doing nice things for your kids, in moderation. Get feedback from Mom first, ask questions, then be quiet and listen. When moms and dads learn to respect each other's values, it almost always ends up a win/win.

When we find ourselves as dads using money to win love, we're in trouble. The best way to fight this is to stop comparing yourself to others and instill in your child a healthy identity not measured by materialism. The propensity for any of us to fall into this trap comes from seeing mere humans as more important than God. When we put the opinions of mankind on a pedestal, we are forging idols in place of God Almighty. In his book, *When People Are Big and God Is Small,* Edward T. Welch says:

> However you put it, the fear of man can be summarized this way: we replace God with people. Instead of a biblically guided fear of the Lord, we fear others. Of course the fear of man goes by other names. When we are in our teens, it's called "peer pressure." When we are older, it is called "people-pleasing." Recently, it's been called "codependency." With these labels in mind, we can spot the fear of man everywhere.[2]

The pressure to be successful in this world is overwhelming. In order to avoid placing our worth and identity in worldly accomplishments or possessions, we must speak truth to ourselves constantly, to remind us who we are in Christ.

The Convertible Dad

This is the guy who is living life for himself, regardless of income or successes. The Convertible Dad is the man who often leaves his kids with a sitter so he can go on a date or out with his buddies. He enjoys being single, and although he loves his kids, he doesn't always like them. They cramp his style. He looks for opportunities to ditch them with a friend while he runs errands. He drops them off at school early and picks them up late. Many children of Convertible Dads are latchkey kids. If he's home for dinner, his children get peanut butter sandwiches while he eats steak. He might be well groomed, but the kids need shoes. He may not do these things on purpose; he's just clueless about his children's welfare. He's either too busy having a blast, or he knows he's falling short so he doesn't even try. Either way, he needs the transforming power of Christ in his life.

As his kids reach adolescence, they begin to see this deficit in their lives. They resent his lifestyle. Often the relationship becomes estranged. It's not a physical, but an emotional abandonment. The

SOUND ADVICE

"You're not a bad parent if you don't save for your kid's college because instead you had to choose to feed them and clothe them. Those things come first. They can go to school and do this thing called 'work' while they're in school."

—Dave Ramsey[3]

father is there—he's just not there *for them*. His lack of attention and care often create the same results we see in those with absent fathers—troubled boys and promiscuous girls. When I worked for the State of Florida as a Law Enforcement Officer, many of the criminals who passed through my supervision were fatherless. A 2002 Department of Justice survey of 7,000 inmates revealed that 39 percent of jail inmates had an uninvolved father when growing up.[4]

The Minivan Dad

Minivan Dad's favorite movies feature hero dads like Will Smith's character in *The Pursuit of Happyness*. He volunteers at school and coaches the neighborhood soccer team. His children's friends love to gather at his home.

At a party, he brings gluten-free desserts and gravitates toward the single moms, discussing the woes of his kid's peanut allergies. He relates to moms. Men don't trust him—women wish they had married him.

This man lives for his kids. He has dedicated his life to becoming the best single dad the world has ever known. His kids feel secure and well cared for, but something is missing. He's lonely and doesn't know it. He's so busy being Super Dad that he's forgotten his own needs. He gets an occasional glimpse of a different life whenever a woman looks at him with a particular type of admiration. Single ladies are all over him like cops on a donut. He likes the attention but quickly dismisses it, all for the sake of the cause: his kids.

It's a noble cause, but because of all the positive affirmation he gets from other adults, this guy often forgets to care for himself first. As discussed in chapters six and seven, we need to remember to keep ourselves tuned-up phys-

"I don't even know how to speak up for myself, because I don't really have a father who would give me the confidence or advice."

—Eminem[5]

ically, spiritually, and emotionally. Otherwise, sooner or later, Minivan Dad is either going to become resentful of his role or abandon it altogether to pursue his own needs and goals. All of us feel the need to develop ourselves on some level. If we go too long without pursuing this, we become either depressed or angry.

The Bible tells us there are seasons for everything. Being a Minivan Dad is sometimes necessary for a season. That's OK; just don't let it define you as a man or a parent. You are more than a minivan. So make time to work within and improve your other gifts and skills.

The Clunker Dad

The Clunker Dad more than likely doesn't have custody of the little ones—by his choice. He's lazy and puts little effort into fatherhood, dreading the kids' arrival. He's an embarrassment to the male gender, sitting on the couch all weekend, never putting on a shirt. He finds reasons to avoid any activity at all and prefers to sleep during his children's weekend visits. He's a bore, and they hate spending time with Clunker Dad. He sends the kids back to Mom with unwashed laundry. He believes child rearing is not his responsibility because he's a man. Kids are a woman's thing, and he makes sure his children know it. That way they won't expect much from him.

The mentality of the Clunker Dad can fall on any one of us at any given time. None of us are above it. When you feel it creeping up on you, kill it by taking a parenting class or something. Stand up, change out of your bathrobe, and take the kids outside to throw a softball. Do something, anything—but don't be lazy. Enough said.

The Electric Mini Dad

This dad lives in an efficiency apartment with a mini fridge. There's nothing homey about it. He's a minimalist, and like the Clunker Dad, he too prefers to let the mother raise the kids. Quick, efficient visits are his preference. He enjoys seeing his kids, but it's usually confined to six or eight hours—no sleepovers and certainly no lengthy summer visits. He has no room for them in his home or his schedule. Electric Mini Dads love being more of a cool uncle figure, rather than a dad, because parenting is a long, drawn-out process with too many loose ends. He needs concise, check-box relationships with high boundaries. On birthdays his kids get a text from him or a card if he's feeling extravagant.

Sadly, the children will sense a lack of belonging early on and beg to stay with Mom. Overcoming the Electric Mini Dad syndrome requires a huge step. This dad has to risk messiness by opening his home and heart to his kids, who will most definitely disturb his world and bring chaos and inefficiency—but it will be wondrous.

The Model T Dad

This father is feeling his years. He longs for the day when his kids become more independent. He is frustrated when his kids talk about newer technology or conversational phrases he doesn't understand. He can't keep up.

The kids get it—their dad is old. They see he's a bit out of touch with their world. Perhaps he's too advanced in years to deal with kids this young. He might even want to slap himself for not thinking all that through before he conceived them. That's unfortunate.

It's OK to feel that way at times; all dads do, no matter their age. As an older father starting a new family in my second marriage, I found it helpful to ask my little girls questions rather than remain clueless. This kept me from being a Model T. When you make an effort to understand your son or daughter's world, they'll appreciate it. It's often pride and fear that keep us from being the dad our kids need. They need a father, not another grandpa.

The Sedan Dad

The Sedan Dad is the man who is just your typical well-rounded dad. He doesn't stick out from the others. He provides well, gives the kids a safe, secure home, and is reliable. The Sedan Dad is the middle of the road car. There is no shame in being a Sedan Dad; it's respectable.

"It is easier for a father to have children, than for children to have a real father."
—Pope John XXIII (1881–1963)[6]

I pray every day for the Lord to make me a Sedan Dad, someone who will glorify God by being the parent he wants me to be. I'm not knocking being unique. Even sedans are different. They can even be above average. Sedans come in different makes, models, and editions—in a myriad of colors. Some have differing gas mileage and various bells and whistles. But they have one thing in common—when running well, they do their job.

My prayer for you and me and every dad, is that the Lord would move us toward greatness as humble Sedans who can get the job done, for the sake of our children and for the glory of God.

CHECKING YOUR GAUGES ——————————————————

Which vehicle dad do you most relate to and why?

How might you be spoiling your kids?

Do you ever find yourself striving to prove something? What is it and why?

Advice from others is a valuable tool. How long has it been since you allowed someone to point out blind spots in your fathering?

STUDYING THE MAP ——————————————————

"Keep your lives free from the love of money and be content with what you have, because God has said, 'Never will I leave you; never will I forsake you.'" Hebrews 13:5 (NIV)

REROUTING

What steps must you take to transform into a Sedan? If you already see yourself as Sedan Dad, what special feature do you need to make you top of the line?

Try various ways to step out of your comfort zone in order to help yourself become a well-rounded parent. Mix it up a little. Spend time asking the kids lots of questions—meaningful inquiries like what they want to be when they grow up. Ask what they fear most about the future and why. Concentrate on knowing one another better.

REFUELING

Dear Heavenly Father, reveal how you want me to change. Help me remember that image is not important and point me back to you. I want people to be small, and I want you to be big. I know you have made me unique. Although you have gifted me in ways I never want to forsake, prod me out of my comfort zone. Help me to keep my focus on you as I raise my kids—teaching them a relationship with you is most important. Help me model godliness, rather than materialism, in all I do. When I am tired, lift me up. When I am lacking, give me resources. When I am clueless, open my eyes. Help me be the dad you have called me to be. Amen.

CHAPTER 11

Taxi!
(Putting Others First)

"Sorry, this cab is taken."

It was winter in France. There on business, I had spent the last two days learning my way around Paris by bus.

This afternoon, however, I missed the bus and had to hire a taxi to get to the hotel. Climbing in, I proceeded to explain the best route. The driver didn't bother to glance back at me. He just pulled away from the curb and grunted something—probably French for "stupid American."

I could've gotten a lot of work done while the driver did his job, but I didn't trust him. We drove right past Notre Dame Cathedral and the Arc de Triomphe, but was I enjoying the view?

Nope.

Instead, I spent the whole thirty minutes sitting on the edge of my seat asking him why he was taking this particular route and staring at the meter on the dashboard. I was sure the city bus would have been better.

We got to the hotel in record time. My inability to adapt cost me much more than the taxi fare. It cost me some work time, some sightseeing opportunities, and most of all, peace of mind.

If you've ever used a taxi or other public wheels, you understand that inexpensive transportation still has its costs. Taxis are a great way of getting from point A to point B. But it requires flexibility and trust.

Single fathering is similar. There may be a season of your single parenting when you'll need to change things up in order to get your family where you want. Your goal might feel sometimes like it's just to get the kids raised into adulthood—from point A to B. However, in order to accomplish this you have to continually find creative, more efficient ways of pointing them toward that final destination—hope and trust in Jesus. Like navigating through a crowded city, you may need to adjust your means of transport in order to get to that destination the best way.

As Christian fathers, our children are our mission field. They are our disciples. There's no greater goal for us as dads than to lead our child toward a lasting relationship with Jesus. But from time to time as our kids mature, we have to adjust our means of getting there.

Nothing explains this better than my observation as a missionary of changing social norms. These days, many people come to know Jesus through relationship with other believers first, not the other way around. As a professional full-time missionary with Cru, I've seen trends change over the years. Our organization is known for being on the cutting edge evangelistically, and we've learned to adjust with the times in order to be more effective in winning, building, and sending new believers. Door-to-door witnessing isn't as popular anymore because society has evolved. People often require relationship first before they'll hear why they need a Savior. It's no different at home; relationship often precedes and segues into spiritual conversations. Consequently, if parents fail to adjust and lose relational ground with their kids, they often forfeit some godly influence over them as well.

So how do you insure a relationship with your child when they don't live near you? What about when outside circumstances prevent that relationship from being nurtured? Many times it's not your fault, but if you've already lost closeness with your son or daughter, there's still time to correct this. Start mending it today, even if it's long distance.

Whether your goal for your family is spiritual or something more domestic like custody issues, if the old plan isn't effective anymore, perhaps it's time to try a taxi.

Backseat Driving

When you climb into a taxi you might be able to suggest the quickest route, but in the end you're not the one behind the wheel, and you quickly learn to relinquish your will in order to let that driver get you to your destination *his* way. No matter the route he takes, when you arrive, you still get what you want—your destination.

In a taxi there's really no use in arguing with the driver. A wise passenger just sits back, enjoys the sights, and waits patiently for the destination to appear. There's going to come a time as a single parent when you must give up your rights in order to keep the peace or get to your goal. It's important to keep telling yourself the goal is to get there; it often doesn't matter *how* you get there. When you get caught up in the "how," then the whole reason you hired a taxi in the first place is lost. You might as well drive your own car.

My former wife and I weren't so smart as we navigated through single parenting. We couldn't enjoy the ride because of our own ideals regarding the best route to take. Many times our desires and wants showed up most aggressively during custody changes. We soon realized visitation for the kids required planning and consideration for one another.

Special occasions were the most difficult. The sense of entitlement was strong, but in the end, one of us had to give in. Those times when we wanted to hold on to something tightly were probably when we needed to let it go the most. I've learned placing others' needs above my own not only thwarts self-absorbed attitudes but also is biblical (Matt. 7:12).

Sharing

Even as a custodial parent, there were no guarantees that special occasions would be celebrated with me. I had to be fair and share these moments with their mother.

During the first few years following the divorce, my ex-wife and I were awarded joint custody, with the children living primarily in their mother's house. However, since we lived in the same town, I was able to house Sharaya and Caleb up to three or four days a week sometimes. It was a great arrangement, allowing me to keep them in church on the weekends and stay active with their school's Parent-Teacher Association.

However, when my former wife decided to move out of state, things got complicated. My children were suddenly three states away, so we had to compromise when it came to holidays. My ex and I could no longer drive the kids to one another's home midday on Thanksgiving or Christmas. Sharing was hard, especially when minor holidays (i.e., Valentine's Day, Father's Day) didn't merit a road trip.

Whether you live close to your child or not, rotating those special occasions will eventually be

TEXT TROUBLE

Sweet16: dad r u coming?

Beerbelly: Overslept. Gonna be late.

Sweet16: OMG U jus woke? It's 3PM! How L8?

Beerbelly: Um, wow that's bad spelling.

Sweet16: it's text dad. supposed 2b brief.

Beerbelly: I killed Mom so she wouldn't worry.

Sweet16: OMG what?

Beerbelly: I called Mom. Stupid auto-fill!!!! Now I'm rolling on the floor laughing.

Sweet16: just type ROFL. UR so lame dad.

Beerbelly: Huh?

Sweet16: nvm. B here soon?

Beerbelly: 20 min

Beerbelly: Nice & short. How cool was that?!

Sweet16: zzzzzzzz

an issue. We need to emotionally prepare ourselves by having a plan. Talking that plan over with their mother is key. Should you rotate every other holiday? What special days do you consider unimportant to be with your child? How does their mother feel about this? What's your child's opinion?

Summer and Christmas

More than likely, the two biggies are summer months and extended Christmas vacations. If you live far from each other, these visits must be agreed upon months in advance, if not already addressed in the original divorce decree.

In most cases, it seems fair to allow the noncustodial parent to have the child over the majority of the summer. At the very least, thirty days. Guys, if you're not usually the custodial parent but you're keeping the kids all summer, this isn't time for a free ride. Continue to pay your child support. I understand it's difficult and seems unfair to continue giving to their mother when you are caring for the kids. Let me gently say—get over it. Yes, it stinks, but it's honorable.

Gentlemen, the mother of your children needs that money to help her catch up on extra expenses she hadn't planned on throughout the year. Besides, you don't want anything to damage your integrity. Allow no ammunition for people to bad-mouth you as a provider. Faithfully pay your child support, and do your best to feed and care for your child while he/she is with you. I started saving up a few months before my kids arrived for the summer. This helped ease the impact on the grocery and utility bills.

Christmas arrangements merited a phone call to my former spouse as well. Not every year was the same. Sometimes I drove up to be with the kids in their own little town on the week of Christmas. Other times they came to me—for the whole two weeks or maybe just a few days. Sometimes I compromised, flying them down for the week *after* Christmas. The beautiful thing about this holiday is America celebrates the whole of December. I never felt cheated as long as I was with the kids at some point during that four-week period to decorate the house, go shopping, open gifts, and have a nice holiday dinner together. Even New Year's Eve is still Christmassy enough to feel satisfied with being together. Choose your battles and learn flexibility.

Making It Memorable

What your family decides the lesser occasions are, will differ from other families. From the day she was born, Valentine's Day usually involved my daughter. When she was little, I got Sharaya a plush toy with candy hearts. As a teenager she continued to get chocolate and a card. I wanted her to know she was my sweetheart. Doing this was my attempt to reinforce that I was her knight, and until she found a husband, she needn't

look elsewhere to feel valued or
loved. Even when we weren't
together for Valentine's Day, I
continued the tradition until she
was engaged to be married. My
son got zip. But I showed Caleb
my love in other, unromantic
ways throughout the year.

Easter is a great time to have
your child with you in church.
I always looked forward to that,
although it didn't always happen

SUMMER TIP

Near the end of a summer create
a photo book online and fill it
with images from everything you
did with the kids that summer.

Present it to them on their last
day or mail it to them afterward.

A flash drive works too, especially if you have movies.

This easily replaces any souvenir you refused to buy them
throughout the summer.

during those seasons when they lived out of state. When they were with
me, it was easy enough to fill an Easter basket or arrange a quick egg
hunt in the back yard. Picnics on July 4th and Labor Day almost always
included swimming. Just make a memory whenever you can, and don't
forget the camera.

Relatives and friends are important too. After a divorce, when a sense
of belonging and identity is so uncertain for kids, I tried to include family for special occasions. It wasn't always possible, as I didn't have many
kin nearby from either side of the tree. However, even hanging out with
church families was memorable for my kids.

Finally, we need to make sure to remind our kids about Mother's Day
at least a week in advance, and again the day before. It doesn't matter how
you feel about Mom—whether you are still madly in love with her or you
think she's a sleazebag—make sure your child honors her.

Birthdays

If you're like me, certain birthdays you just don't want to miss, especially those older years. The bad thing is, those are the birthdays when you
begin to notice they have made plans that don't necessarily include Dad.
That can be painful, but it has nothing to do with you. It's about them
growing up. Don't take it personally.

Milestone birthdays are different for every family. Whatever they are, make it special even from a distance. If you can't be there in person, think of ways an average phone call can stand out

SUGGESTED MILESTONE BIRTHDAYS:
1st, 5th, 10th, 13th, 16th, 18th, 21st

among the rest. Try including a treasure hunt for a special gift you hid during your last visit. Mail a video with a special message. Talk with their mother about rights-of-passage gifts. If possible, decide together when it's time for your daughter's first Barbie. Discuss ahead of time the appropriate age for your daughter's (or son's) ears to be pierced.

I know some of us don't have the luxury of cordial discussions with our former spouse. I know firsthand, some gifts and ceremonies aren't always up for discussion if the parents are antagonistic toward one another. Tattoos and other irreversible decisions might be implemented without our input. Just take a deep breath and turn your attention toward the celebration of your child's special day—that's what matters.

In turn, we too must remember to be considerate. Buying a car for your child's sixteenth birthday without talking to Mom first is a no-no. The same for letting them go to what you might think is an innocent concert. Some things might be legal but not necessarily profitable. Know your former spouse's convictions on certain issues. Put yourself in Mom's shoes before doing something that, for you, may just be a simple token. The marriage may have ended, but your joint parenting hasn't. We have to learn to separate the two relationships we have with our former spouse. The marriage relationship is over and dead, whereas the joint parenting relationship will continue until one of you is deceased. You may not want to ask permission about something, but you must, regardless of whether you're antagonistic or amiable. Discuss, discuss, and discuss some more.

Gifts can cause more fights between parents than ever imagined, especially if one parent tries to out give the other. There's nothing worse than observing divorced parents trying to one-up each other with expensive or sometimes inappropriate presents.

When we can learn to take a backseat and roll with the changes, the peace this brings can help everyone enjoy the journey just a bit more.

CHECKING YOUR GAUGES

What special occasion do you feel should always be *your* day to have custody? Why do you feel so strongly about this?

How do feelings of entitlement affect your integrity, maturity, fatherhood, and spiritual influence on others?

How long has it been since you surrendered control and embraced change in order to achieve a better outcome (i.e., peace)?

STUDYING THE MAP

"Love is patient and kind; love does not envy or boast; it is not arrogant or rude. It does not insist on its own way; it is not irritable or resentful." 1 Corinthians 13:4–5

REROUTING

Start discussions with your ex-spouse now about the next special occasion. Reflect on some past special occasions when a conflict arose due to unmet expectations. Consider how you might die to self by initiating an apology to your children's mother.

REFUELING

Dear Heavenly Father, I know there are holidays when I hold tightly to my opinion that my child should be with me. Help me to consider others and not myself. Give me wisdom when planning, and create a spirit of humility in me. Help me place others' needs ahead of my own desires and learn to be an easy adapter. Amen.

CHAPTER 12

Fuzzy Dice
(Rethinking Traditions)

"More construction! Are you kidding me?"

As a young teen, I loved movies. So when I was finally able to drive I saw a cute little Chewbacca toy I could hang from my rearview mirror and I had to have it.

Thus began a decade of hanging things from my mirror that represented a piece of my identity. When I graduated high school, the tassel from my hat was displayed. In college, I swapped it out for a Rubik's Cube. When I married at twenty-one, I decided it was time to grow up. So I hung my wife's wedding garter on my mirror. My young bride and I were clueless and thought it was a cool tradition. What was I thinking? I might as well have hung her panties in the window. Was there no older man in my life brave enough to slap some sense into me?

People often do things they laugh about later. Whether it's a copstache or skinny jeans, we try new things. They either work or they don't, and it's no big deal. It's when they don't work yet we refuse to let them go, that we need an intervention.

We've Always Done It

I once heard a story about a husband who was watching his wife prepare a leg of lamb. She sawed off several inches from the shank bone, and when she finished he asked why she'd cut it off. "Does it taste better that way?"

"I don't really know, my mum taught me how to cook. She always did it like this."

The man couldn't stop wondering about it, so he asked his mother-in-law.

She said, "I don't really know why I do it. My mom did it that way. I'm curious too. Let me call and ask her."

The woman got on the phone and asked her aging mother the same question. On the other end of the line the old woman burst into laughter. "It's just because my pan was too short!"

This little story illustrates the power of an unquestioned tradition. Whether good or bad—or in this case, just plain unnecessary—we often carry traditions without evaluating the value and meaning behind them.

CHRISTMAS TRADITION IDEAS FOR THE KIDS

Open one gift (maybe new PJs) a day early.

Each year, buy a new ornament for the tree together.

Buy a gingerbread house kit and build it together.

Get fast-food gift certificates for a homeless person.

Get in the car and drive to three friends' homes, then sing carols on their doorsteps.

Cram in as many holiday movies as you can watch together before Christmas.

Have the kids put coal in their mother's stocking (I'm joking).

Do You Hear What I Hear?

It seems like a lifetime ago. This particular year it was my ex-wife's turn to enjoy spending Christmas with the kids. I had arranged with her to let me call our kids early that morning and wake them to our special holiday song. For several Christmases prior to the divorce, the kids had awakened at 7:00 a.m. to a joyous carol and Daddy shouting, "Ho Ho Ho! Merry Christmas!"

My kids stumbled to the phone. It only took a moment for the fun music to cut through their sleepy haze and induce a giggle or two from their lips. Before long I found myself turning down the music and speaking in quiet tones about memories of past holidays. We talked about being together next Christmas. What started as a rather exciting wake-up call quickly became a tender moment.

After listening to them squeal over the gifts I mailed, I reminded them how much they were loved and missed. Then I hung up.

Holding traditions—however lame they might be—is important to the security and well-being of children who have been uprooted due to divorce or separation. Whether we live with our kids or not, we need to be diligent in helping our children keep a sense of identity and belonging. My kids were fortunate to have a mother who allowed such an invasion of privacy. Let's face it, we shouldn't expect our ex-spouse to continue holding to traditions that could be painful or even irritating for her to continue. It may be easy when our kids are with us, but what can a noncustodial parent do to ensure a tradition continues when everything seems to work against that? Perhaps not all traditions need to survive.

I had to learn to review the importance of some events. Was watching the Macy's Thanksgiving Day Parade truly a tradition, or simply a boring habit? Was it something I felt obligated to fulfill each year because my parents did it? Often I had to count the cost of keeping a tradition versus ditching it. It's critical to make sure our traditions play a role in providing each family member—including us dads—with a distinctiveness that reinforces identity. Trying to keep our own memories alive may not be a valid enough reason to make it happen for our own kids. The same goes for a religious tradition. Sometimes attending a Christmas Eve candlelight service can feel so important that it causes us to condemn ourselves if we skip it.

If a particular ritual is an important part of our family history, we may merely need to tweak the tradition a bit to fit our new lifestyle. If it's possible, discussing its importance with our ex-spouse can help. It could be we need to postpone an event until our kids are with us again.

Today my son and daughter are grown, but they still recall that special song every Christmas morning, whether we were together or apart. It helped them feel secure, defined our family, and had a small part in giving us our uniqueness.

Your former spouse also has traditions that don't necessarily include you. It's not all about you and the kids. There's another parent involved, and they are learning to adjust traditions too.

New Traditions

I used to live in Australia. I loved the culture and made some very dear, lifelong friends. The language, however, took me a while to understand. Although they speak English, the words had entirely different meanings, as revealed during my first Aussie footy game.

"Who should I be rooting for?" I wanted my Aussie friends to help me cheer the right team.

"Shhh! Tez, we don't use that term here," Lachlan whispered. The others with us giggled.

"Why? Wha—?"

He leaned in, laughing, "*Root* means the f-word, Mate. We just say cheering or barracking."

My face turned a beautiful burgundy as my mouth dropped.

I've worn many hats over the years as a missionary with Cru. During the years my family and I were assigned to reach Australia with the gospel, I served as editor-in-chief for a Cru magazine. The first lesson I needed to master was the subtleties of the language. Just like British English isn't the same as South African or Canadian English, so it goes with the dialects Down Under versus the States. My American grammar and spelling norms stuck out like pins in a balloon factory. Flexibility is key for cross-cultural ministry, so if I couldn't write or edit the articles like an Aussie, we'd lose readership. An attitude of "in the USA we do it like this . . ." just wouldn't fly. Recruiting a team of Aussies around me, I quickly assimilated by letting go of my country's traditional rules of writing.

You will be surprised at how quickly old traditions fade into oblivion when new memories are birthed. Quite by accident one New Year's Eve, my children and I invented a brand new tradition by mutual consent. Now there's an idea—let the kids decide for a change. Sharaya and Caleb were excited to be up so late. It was five minutes before midnight, and we were alone watching the countdown on television. I made root beer floats, and we snuggled together on the couch.

"This is the best New Year ever, Daddy," grinned my daughter. "Let's do this every year."

Some new habits require more time for our children to adopt. Traditions that come from new partners, stepparents, or siblings from blended families are especially fragile. We can't expect immediate acceptance of new traditions, especially if the child is older.

I was an older teenager when my mother died. It was hard for me to see my father's new wife settle into our home less than a year later. I was looking forward to pulling out Mom's ornaments and special decorations. It would be healing to see memories of my mother around the house during this first Christmas without her.

It never happened.

Unlike Mom, she didn't care for Christmas trees. Her holiday décor around the house was understated and hard to spot. She planned a quiet, low-key gathering on Christmas Eve. We'd never opened gifts that early; we always waited until Christmas morning. *Who did this woman think she was?*

I survived; there are worse things to be angry about. My new stepmother ended up being quite nice, but neither she nor my father had a clue about my turmoil. My point is, be sensitive, fathers.

Many times, we may have no idea what story or memory is linked to a special tradition. The last thing we want to do is appear as if we're trying to snuff-out someone's memory. It's a great idea to ask our kids' opinions first. Not that we have to coddle them, but never assume a child is OK with replacing a favorite ornament of a missing parent. Remember, it's about security and a sense of belonging for them. We want to keep that as best we can.

With my own children I tried to be sensitive to provide a warm and familiar blanket of identity. Traditions don't always have to be deep and meaningful. Some of the most fun rituals are the ones that hold no special memory except that it's just plain crazy.

Letting It Die

Whether it's an Easter basket, a water balloon fight on
Independence Day, or Chuck
E. Cheese's for a birthday, some
traditions will eventually be
outgrown—that's life. However,
they don't have to be forgotten.
Talking about them is all you

SURVIVING FATHER'S DAY ALONE

Plan the day. Don't mope.
Call the kids if they haven't called
    you by 5:00 p.m.
Write a letter to them.
Celebrate your own father.
Have dinner with other single
    dads.

need sometimes to stir up a warm discussion or a belly laugh.

As my kids became teenagers, the day came when I couldn't wake
them on Christmas morning with a mere "Ho Ho Ho!" The loud
music eventually became obnoxious, and I had to let the tradition rest
in peace. By then, I think we were all relieved.

I could have lit a ca ndle and stared at it, pining over the absence
of my kids or the death of a great tradition. I can certainly relate with
you dads who never get a birthday card or a phone call initiated by
Junior on Father's Day. I understand why single dads spend the day
crying in their beer or blogging about it until their fingers are sore. I
get it, I do.

It stinks, and I have no advice except we need to just get our minds
off it and stop trying to decorate that rearview mirror. Call a friend,
go to a movie, play some Ultimate Frisbee with other single dads, or
something—but you're going to have to embrace the change.

CHECKING YOUR GAUGES

What special tradition do you feel defensive over?

Why do you feel so strongly about it?

How does your child react to particular traditions?

Could it be time to throw away those fuzzy dice (a.k.a., unnecessary traditions)?

STUDYING THE MAP ─────────────────────────────

"Do nothing from selfish ambition or conceit, but in humility count others more significant than yourselves." Philippians 2:3

REROUTING ──────────────────────────────────

Ask your children what traditions they most appreciate and why. Ask what they would change about holiday visits and why.

REFUELING ──────────────────────────────────

God, please give me creativity when it comes to finding new traditions and wisdom to know when other traditions should be retired. Lord, in the end, what matters is that I spend time with my child. Help me protect that truth and to direct more of my energies toward demonstrating the love of Jesus to my child. Amen.

CHAPTER 13

Selling the Minivan
(Preparing for an Empty Nest)

"Gross! How long has this diaper been under my seat?"

"Caleb wants to live with you again." My ex-wife released a sigh.

I pulled the phone away and fist-pumped, trying to keep the smile from being detected in my voice. "Oh? What's that about?"

"He misses you, and to be honest, he needs you in his life. He's been very disrespectful and aggressive lately."

"That's not good. Is he still allowed to listen to gangsta rap?"

She released another heavy sigh, ignoring my question.

"You know it influences his view of women." I found myself getting angry. Not because Caleb's mother was letting him absorb questionable lyrics, but because my son should not be treating his mother that way.

We agreed our eleven-year-old needed a positive male role model in his life on a daily basis. I wanted to seize the opportunity before his mother retracted it, so I quickly arranged for Caleb to come live with my room-mate and me in Florida.

Losing Caleb

A few years earlier, my ex-wife had moved out of state with my chil-dren, and I went through several years of on-again/off-again custodial parenting. Each time the kids reenrolled in a new school, they lost friends, their grades suffered, and their sense of stability suffered. They also faced adjustments between a Christian and non-Christian household. At one point I filed for a custody change, in light of some inappropriate activities I observed.

I lost the case.

I didn't want to go through that again. Although I knew the social and academic toll this would take on my son, I allowed it. Probably a big mistake, but in the interest of time, I skipped modifying our agreement legally.

Immediately collecting Caleb and his belongings, I brought him into my home. I hoped to influence Caleb and create a tighter bond by having him full-time again.

My time with Caleb was precious. We grew close, and I can't remember ever needing to punish him. He was the most delightful, funny, well-behaved kid a guy could ask for.

We went to church together, cleaned the house together, and enjoyed scratching and burping with no one to scold us. The rewards far outweighed the cost.

If it were a movie, this would be the part where a montage is shown, backed by an '80s rock ballad and ending with the two of us in our boxers playing air guitars.

School ended and Caleb wanted to visit his mother for a month. I thought that would be a grand idea. She missed him, and it would give them time to reconnect.

Four weeks later came a phone call from his mother informing me he wouldn't be returning. Although I knew this might happen, my risky move backfired. Hurt and discouragement flooded in.

The house felt so empty. I felt like a parent who loses a child in an accident; Caleb was here, then suddenly gone. Walking by his room I'd stare at his bed. His clothes were still hanging in the closet, and I would sniff them just to get a whiff of my son. I wondered if the residuals of my divorce would continue to rise up and slap my heart.

Chin Up!

When Caleb left, I struggled. My protective instincts ran amok and I was angry. Sure I enjoyed more freedom, but I worried how Caleb was fairing. Thankfully, I had a community of people from my small group who surrounded me.

The church I attended at the time was passionate about small home-based groups. I plugged into one of the healthiest groups in the church. It was multigener-

7 REASONS YOU NEED A SMALL GROUP

1. It was Jesus's model.
2. It was the early church's model.
3. These relationships make you spiritually mature.
4. It offers an outlet for you to minister to others.
5. You'll make friends for life!
6. It's fun and you need some fun.
7. You'll never understand until you try it.

ational and contained married and single members who loved each other dearly. They walked with me through the temporary crisis. Without that love and support I surely would have shut down when Caleb left.

Don't get me wrong; the Lord really is all we need. But I believe we sell community short when we assume all our needs will be met solely by our Heavenly Father. I'm not saying he can't do it. I'm saying he sometimes won't, because he often chooses to use community—other humans—to reveal his heart for us.

Men, I've said it before, we need community. Don't wait for a crisis before you surround yourself with other believers. Find that group now, so that when you go through a trial—and trials will come, they always do—you'll have those friends already intricately woven into your life.

So what about the church that doesn't have such dynamic expressions for fellowship? Do something, anything, with others. Don't let life just happen. Be strategic in filling that empty space that used to be occupied with your child's presence. Fill it with the Holy Spirit, then top it off with community.

And stop smelling your kid's clothes. Weirdo!

Losing Sharaya

About a year after my son moved back to his mother's house, I met and eventually married Christine. A few months after the wedding, my children's mother called again. Fifteen-year-old Sharaya refused to attend school and her mother felt it would be beneficial to send her to us. Christine loved my kids, and they loved her, so we jumped at the chance.

We adjusted to life as newlyweds with a teen. Christine even home-schooled Sharaya, helping her catch up academically. Yet after a year, this arrangement also ended, and my daughter moved back to her mother, leaving another hole. This time I had a spouse to grieve with me, but the pain was no less sharp.

Honestly, I don't think I'd do anything differently. I could have hired a lawyer every time my ex and I agreed to swap custodial roles. That would have been the proper way to avoid so much shifting. But for our family situation, I waived expensive legal counsel in order to avoid the stress of court dates. That time and effort was better spent just being Daddy. I'm not recommending this strategy for everyone. Our family opted for this route in order to keep peace and serenity in our homes. Even though it must be implemented sometimes, no one wins when custody turns into a battle to determine who is more fit.

Sharaya and Caleb became old enough to make their own choices about who to live with. I decided from then on, to sell the minivan, fig-uratively speaking. I couldn't allow my son and daughter to constantly move back and forth. It was hard, but for the sake of their school grades and their stability, I knew they must stay with only one of us at least until graduation.

You and I can count on one thing for sure. Even if we never switch cus-tody, our children will grow up and leave. Whether they go back to Mom or off to college, we'll eventually have to sell the minivan. The empty nest can be hell or it can be heaven. What we do with that season of our life rests on us.

As I'm typing this, my fourth child, seven-year-old Anicah, came in and asked me what I'm writing about. I told her I'm sharing ways to help dads make the best of an empty nest.

She shook her head, "Just tell them go have fun and forget about it for a while."

Out of the mouths of babes.

What Now?

Men, you're going to experience some unusual things when your children fly the coop. How you respond can make a difference as to whether your offspring returns to visit or finds excuses to stay away.

Anticipation. Excitement could be the first thing to hit you. You begin to consider what life will look like when your kids are gone. Freedom may induce a little guilt. Don't let it. Embrace the excitement, for it's far better than dread when it comes to saying good-bye.

Regret. That seems to be a dad's favorite go-to emotion whenever we attempt to review our years as a father. Let me encourage you, fellow brothers. Stop listening to Hollywood or whoever else might be saying you're a screw-up at fathering. The Accuser, Satan, wants nothing more than to fill your head with lies and plug your ears from hearing the voice of our Redeemer, Jesus Christ. Sure we've made mistakes, but God is bigger. Hold up that head and allow the Holy Spirit to speak truth into your heart.

Denial. Ignoring the obvious can be evident if you're one of those parents who refuses to remove anything from the house. After years of having the kids return to me over and over, I felt like this empty nest would never be final. I knew I moved forward when I packed up both Sharaya's and Caleb's baby books and childhood art projects. Reserving a few framed photos of them to set around the house, I stored everything else in the attic. With a sigh, my denial was over.

New Interests. You might find you're suddenly engrossed in your career. That's a normal and healthy reaction after your brood has fled the household. Go with it. You may also find yourself finally interested (if you haven't been already) in pursuing a romantic relationship. That's OK too, but be careful here that you're not just rebounding from the loss of your kids.

Finances. Many dads find they can suddenly spend differ-

> "Fathers–and parents in general– should use the opportunity to re- assess their lives. Take advantage of the slowdown, rediscover marriage, concentrate on getting in shape or entertaining more. The possibilities are endless when you have less responsibility."
> —Susan Yara[1]

ently, especially those of you who've paid child support but now your kid is grown. It's like getting a raise! For men who are full-time custodial fathers, a bit more padding may be in *your* wallet as well. Even if paying for Junior's university expenses, there's still the benefit of lower utilities and knowing that your last few Oreos are still waiting for you in the pantry. Those few extra bucks can be the doorway to lifestyle changes. Whether it's a long-awaited mission trip or moving into a hip part of town, be free to enjoy life.

During this transition it can be easy to feel like you're the only one experiencing shift. Your kids are too, whether they know how to express this or not. Remind them that they haven't slipped from your radar. Set up a time to regularly call them. If they're busy and not always available—that's just life. At least you're doing your part to stay connected. In a moment of insecurity, I once asked my grown son if I called him at a bad time.

"Dad," he chuckled, "if I'm busy hanging with my friends, I'm not gonna answer the phone. If I don't feel like talking to you, I won't."

How's that for speaking truth? That's one of the things I love about Caleb. The big twerp is so confident about the depth of our relationship that he can speak his mind anytime, knowing it will never alter my love for him.

Whatever you choose to do with your extra time and money, remember to just be you. Allow yourself to shed the title of Tommy's daddy. Learn to glorify God during this new season by being all he has created you to be outside of parenting.

The Empty Car Seat

There are seasons of parenting when you don't always need to sell the minivan. If the empty nest is temporary you may just need to remove the car seat until they return. But if you've had a child outgrow a car seat, you know it brings mixed feelings. A part of you is excited to claim your back seat again. You remove the safety chair and clean the car's upholstery. It feels good to get rid of those stale Cheerios and orange fish crackers. But there's another part of you that's sad to see it go; it feels like the end of an era.

I love my kids. No one can ever say I didn't grieve when they moved out. Likewise, when they got too big even to spend summers with me, I ached to see them. Yet there came a time when I knew I needed to stop making their bedroom a shrine and turn it into something more practical. At first I felt guilty for replacing their beds with a computer desk and filing cabinets. What if they were to visit and had to sleep on a couch? Would they feel erased?

Phhht!

There goes that familiar guilt trip. I soon realized my kids didn't base my love on how many beds I had in my house.

Removing those virtual car seats, I began to make plans for myself. I decided to pursue things I'd put on hold for years. I wanted to study French, learn to play guitar, be in a community play. Like a commuter who listens to audio books while driving, I made the best of my spare time, developing myself so I could become a more interesting, well-rounded person.

For me, that season didn't last long. I found love again and got married. My new bride, Christine, became pregnant and before long I started raising a family all over again. I didn't mind. I was about to experience fatherhood in an entirely different way.

CHECKING YOUR GAUGES ————————————————

How have you prepared yourself mentally for an expected or unexpected separation from your kids?

In what ways might you have unintentionally built your life to revolve too much around your children?

STUDYING THE MAP

"For everything there is a season, and a time for every matter under heaven:
a time to be born, and a time to die;
a time to plant, and a time to pluck up what is planted;
a time to kill, and a time to heal;
a time to break down, and a time to build up;
a time to weep, and a time to laugh;
a time to mourn, and a time to dance;
a time to cast away stones, and a time to gather stones together;
a time to embrace, and a time to refrain from embracing;
a time to seek, and a time to lose;
a time to keep, and a time to cast away;
a time to tear, and a time to sew;
a time to keep silence, and a time to speak;
a time to love, and a time to hate;
a time for war, and a time for peace."
Ecclesiastes 3:1–8

REROUTING

Getting things out in the open eliminates surprises. Set aside time to discuss with your child their feelings about living with or visiting you.

As difficult as it might be, at least once yearly, you and your ex-spouse need to discuss any possible changes either of you foresee in the near future regarding living arrangements for your child. Remember, some changes should be made legal with the court system if your child is younger than eighteen.

Who do you have to support you during those times you are absent from your kids?

List three things you'd like to do for yourself when your nest is empty.

REFUELING

Dear Father, I want to glorify you in every season of my life. I know if you see fit, you can choose to take my child from me at any time. Whether they are taken or they leave on their own accord, help me trust your sovereignty. Give me wisdom to know if I should fight or let you be my defender. Your plans are more strategic than mine because you've already seen what the future holds. Please help me make the most of my free time when my child is gone. Lead me in how I should develop myself to be the best at what you created me to be. Draw me, Holy Spirit, that I might spend more time at Jesus's feet and glorify God in every area of my life. In Christ's holy name I pray. Amen.

CHAPTER 14

The Rental
(Dating Again)

"Yes. I'll take the full insurance option, please."

I struggled for quite a while with the idea of dating after my divorce. I didn't feel released for a long time, wondering if my ex might repent and return, yet I didn't desire remarriage at all. In fact, I didn't really trust women anymore.

I know there are many views and interpretations about what Scripture teaches regarding divorce and remarriage. I don't feel a need to address each of those. That's not what this book is for. I encourage you to study Scripture for yourself and seek wisdom from the spiritual authorities in your life. On our own we often make Scripture say what we want it to say. We need godly leaders to confirm what the Holy Spirit may be revealing to us or to redirect our hearts toward truth. For my particular circumstance, 1 Corinthians 7 made it pretty clear I was allowed to remarry. My pastors agreed.

Still, that didn't mean a lot because the desire to marry wasn't present. Not until I was completely content with the idea of being single again and celibate the rest of my life did the Lord allow me to meet Christine.

Dating Kissed Me Good-bye

No wonder she left me for a younger guy.

I looked at myself in the mirror. At thirty-six it was evident my hair was either turning gray or turning loose. I sure didn't feel date-worthy. There's nothing quite as castrating as being rejected by your wife. In an effort to feel hot again, a guy can unwittingly look for approval and worth in the arms of a new romance.

ON DATING NON-CHRISTIANS

"Do not be unequally yoked with unbelievers. For what partnership has righteousness with lawlessness? Or what fellowship has light with darkness?"
—2 Corinthians 6:14

I'm not talking about sex outside of marriage. I trust you already understand as a Christian, that's not permissible. God's Word is clear on this topic. I'm talking about dating too soon. The search for an ego stroke can cause us to engage in some uncharacteristic actions. We men can find ourselves flirting with anyone willing to throw us a compliment. We might consider dating women we wouldn't normally go for, even settle for a nonbeliever—all for a chance at feeling sexy again.

I've heard that it typically takes a person about five years to recover from a divorce. That includes emotional and financial recovery. I'd say that's true in my experience. Although I attempted dating after only two years, I wasn't fully ready to have a healthy courtship until about five years of singleness. Don't be discouraged. That's not a criterion for every father. Each guy comes through that season of singleness differently. But if aiming for five years helps delay your dating even a year or two, then it's worthwhile. Some of us need that time to mend. Otherwise, it's like trying to snow ski with a broken leg. You might be able to rig a device so you can snap your cast into the ski. You might even make it to the bottom of the hill without falling. But your experience won't be the same as if you'd waited until you were fully healed.

Far too many of my male friends have jumped right into a new relationship while rebounding from a divorce. I've seen them date around, leaving a trail of destruction for themselves and others.

Hertz, Doesn't It?

NO COMPROMISE

If you are not officially divorced with the papers in hand, then you are still married to your spouse.

Legally and biblically you are committing unfaithfulness by dating others before a divorce is finalized.

I slid into the driver's seat and turned on the ignition. It was my first time in this car, so I took my time exploring where everything was before I shifted into drive. I tried all the knobs and switches, adjusted the mirrors and steering wheel. Then I got out and looked carefully at the condition of the exterior. This wasn't my vehicle; it was a rental. I needed to return it to the lot in the same condition. This car did not belong to me, someone cared about this car, and how I treated it mattered.

I believe we'd have a lot less carnage among Christian singles if when dating, we men would treat our sisters in Christ more like borrowed valuables. When you understand that something isn't really yours, you tend to treat it more carefully. As with rental cars, you want to present your sister back to the Lord in the same condition as before you arrived. If you decide she is not the woman you're to marry, you want to have treated her in such a way that you can look her future husband in the face unashamed.

Over the years while a single dad, I met some potential wives. But I was scared. Gun shy, I spent a long while learning their character. I watched how they responded to stress, signs of emotional baggage they might carry, and even their relationships with other males. When we decided God wasn't calling us to matrimony, I'd like to think we parted ways with hearts intact. Sadly, we didn't always protect each other's emotions as we should have. We tried to woo one another with gifts, tender touches, romantic cards—even kissing.

Wait, so what's wrong with kissing? It's innocent enough, right?

I'd like to suggest an alternative to what we now consider the classic American dating ritual. I'm passionate about this ideal, although I'm first to admit it doesn't always work flawlessly. I know my opinion is going to be about as popular as a power outage on Super Bowl Sunday, but I have to say it. In my opinion, the accepted norms of today's modern dating rituals are full of unspoken promises that are rarely fulfilled, and the system is in need of a complete overhaul. These innocent acts of romanticism need to be saved if not for marriage then at the very least, for an engagement after a proposal. Wow, I sound so absolutely boring, don't I?

This might sting a little, but if you're a gentleman who's treated your sister in Christ with honor, you shouldn't have dozens of romantic memories to erase if you break up. Nor should you experience how good it feels to embrace her, smell her hair, stroke her face, or look deeply into her eyes. A man who protects his heart and his date's heart won't know how soft her lips feel against his. If you say good-bye, what becomes of all those shoeboxes filled with dreamy letters or poetry? We are forced to admit they were all premature, then wipe it away as if it never happened.

If I had moved with more integrity, I would have helped my lady friends save all those nonsexual emotional intimacies for their future husbands—whether it be me or not.

If you're participating in some of these activities with a woman you're dating, stop it. If you don't end up marrying her, you're delving into romantic conversations and actions not meant to be experienced with anyone but a spouse. First Timothy 5:1–2 instructs us to treat women like our sisters. Protect her heart, for your sake and the sake of your siblings in the Lord.

What's Left?

So how then does one court? If so many innocent things we do to show affection are stumbling blocks, how can we show a lady we are interested in her?

We don't. We only *tell* her.

In my opinion, I'm not fully convinced it's time to show her yet. Save the romance for the engagement. Before a first date you might want to have a conversation that defines the relationship. If you have been up front from the start, you should have already explained you see her as a potential life mate. Invite her to explore that idea together, through group activities and limited dating. This may seem cold and contractual, but this really isn't the time to feel things. It's a time to be logically moving, either toward or away from each other.

You romantics are probably hissing at me right about now. You'll get over it. Tuck your poetry away for now and stay analytical. You often can't trust emotions. Real as they may be, they often cloud your judgment.

Do You Like Me or Not?

So what about that poor woman who expects you to show some attraction to her? After all, the norm is for your affections to

SEVEN EASY WAYS TO DEFRAUD

1. Chat on the phone for hours late at night, especially if you're lying down.
2. Allow her to wash/fold your laundry, especially your underwear.
3. Buy her romantic cards, flowers, or jewelry.
4. Do house repairs for her like a husband would.
5. Let her kiss or hug on your child.
6. Do anything that feels like you're playing house. Take naps and showers while visiting each other's home.
7. Make sure you have no end time for your dates. Let them go on indefinitely.

be easily seen and decipherable. If she can't get a good read from you, she's going to walk. So it's important you continually remind her in other ways that you're shielding her heart and yours. While she might find it refreshing not to deal with all the emotional dating games, she still needs to know there's hope one day of a romantic man appearing behind all that armor. Paint a vision for her of what your relationship will look like if it leads to an engagement. Communication on the front end is a key point in making this stage of the relationship work. Without that, you might feel like a couple of robots walking toward an arranged marriage.

Regretfully, I wasn't always a shining example of decency. I was often guilty of wooing in subtle ways. My desire to display sex appeal trumped efforts to guard my lady friend's affections. An ardent gaze, a lingering touch, a greeting card that said too much. Too often my ego wrestled for attention, leaving chivalry trampled and sucking mud on the road to nobility. As I sheepishly returned my lady friends to God, those all too intimate moments showed up like dings and scratches on a rental car.

Eventually I learned the decency of breaking off a relationship in such a way that we could remain cordial and polite. If this isn't the case, then you'll probably find yourselves avoiding each other. If spotting her in a crowd makes you uncomfortable, you more than likely need to ask forgiveness for inappropriate intimacy. Go and quickly make it right with her.

A successful courtship will have nothing lingering that has defrauded or manipulated either party. Let me be first to admit that's easier said than done, especially if the woman doesn't hold your same values. Although, in this case you may reconsider if this is the right woman for you. I know it's not a perfect world; let's at least aim for a like-minded woman.

I once asked a teenage boy who was interested in my daughter, "If you don't see marriage on the near horizon, why are you asking to date my girl?"

This makes me sound awful, but if a guy can't support a wife and provide a home for her, maybe he should go back to his video games. As a dad, I want my kids to find a spouse, not go window-shopping. Dating and courting are not meant merely for social fun or carefree no-strings-attached interaction with the opposite sex. That's what school playgrounds are for. There's no reason to court any woman you are not seriously considering as a potential wife. Why bother, except that you're using someone to fill a void?

The word *date* or *dating* no longer feels right rolling off my tongue like it used to when I was a teenager. The concept of old-fashioned courting appealed to me as an adult. I needed others involved that would watch over me and my potential wife. I had already been around the block, and I really wasn't into the games that dating insists you play. If I wanted to get to know a woman, it was because I considered her a potential wife, so I made my intentions unmistakable.

I began searching for different values in a woman. Oh, I still enjoyed a pretty face, but I was looking more for a Proverbs 31 woman who ran her household well. A businesswoman who was sharp and independent. A woman who was emotionally mature with healthy boundaries. One who would be a godly mother for my children.

What About the Kids?

In the movie *The Holiday* Jude Law plays the role of Graham, a widower and single dad. To ensure his little girls didn't develop unrealistic hopes of getting a mom from his one-night stands, Graham is committed to keeping his dates and daughters separated to avoid complicated attachments. It's admirable of Graham, despite his promiscuity.

My friend Matt started dating a year after his divorce. "I kept it private—away from my daughter's attention. After a few dates I realized I wasn't ready to pursue a relationship. I dedicated myself to my job and to parenting Brandi. I didn't start seeing women again until she was in high school. By then, she was mature enough to support my decision to date."

I see the wisdom in guarding the hearts of my children against immature hopes or expectations. Albeit there were times when I allowed a potential wife to interact with my children, still I had a few small boundaries in place so as not to defraud my kids. As my relationship with Christine blossomed, it would have been easy to let her and my son draw close. On one particular afternoon it just felt good to see her greet Caleb with a hug and nonchalantly kiss the top of his head. But this presented a problem that I didn't want to address. Christine and I had not agreed yet that we were beyond a shadow of a doubt being called by God into a marriage covenant. If we were to decide against marriage, where had we taken Caleb's heart and how would that break affect him? For the sake of my son, I asked Christine not to show physical affection toward my son until after we were sure of our own path.

Slow Down

Eventually you may want to introduce a girlfriend to your child. This probably shouldn't be an impulsive decision. It's not a verdict made between you and your lady friend during an emotional high, which might go something like this:

"I've got an idea, Bunny. Let's go show you off to the kids right now. I just know they're gonna love you."

"But Bob, we've only gone out three times."

"It's Brett actually, not Bob."

"Oh yeah, sorry." Snapping her gum and twisting her hair.

"So waddaya say?"

"Aren't they with your ex tonight?"

"Who cares! Let her see what a catch you are, Dollface."

"OMG, I'm not really into kids, but OK. Just for a minute though, these stilettos are killin' me."

You know how the story ends. You see it coming. The idiot dad, the clueless girlfriend, the kids silently shaking their heads. Mom's trying to hold back a laugh. It's not pretty.

Please don't be that man.

Don't introduce your child to a temporary acquaintance. But if you've approached this relationship with serious intentions, that's significant. By now she's become a good friend who might be your future wife. So introducing her to family members is proper and expected.

Discovering if God is calling the two of you together toward matrimony requires strategic planning. Your son or daughter needs to know about the introduction ahead of time, so he or she can emotionally prepare to meet their potential stepmom. It's kind of a big deal.

Kids can be an easy read. Often it takes just a moment to watch their reaction and know what they think of someone. If you've taken the time to watch your child's expressions (rather than constantly staring at your lady friend), you'll notice a myriad of facial clues that can help you predict the trajectory of this relationship.

We fear being clueless and blamed for our child's demise. Fairy tales have given us ample fodder for second-guessing our discernment of a spouse. News headlines too are filled with stories of abuse at the hands of a malicious stepparent. It can cause any father to display a lack of trust in God. Everyone's afraid of blindly marrying a serial killer. So we ask ourselves time and again, "Do the kids approve?"

In the end, whether or not your child endorses this lady may not mean so much. Whether toddler or teen, your child's response doesn't ultimately determine who your spouse will be. We have to remember they are immature and aren't always capable of making informed decisions. There's a reason, after all, why kids aren't allowed to vote in elections. The determination for marriage is between you, your girlfriend, and the Lord—and hopefully, a bunch of other believers who are speaking into your life. Your child's opinion can change faster than Justin Bieber's Twitter status.

Trust the Lord.

What If It's My Ex-Wife?

You hear from time to time of those who get back together after a divorce. I'll preface what I'm about to say with this: the opportunity arose in my own divorce but the motive was wrong. Suffice it to say I didn't pursue the offer on biblical grounds. If the opportunity for you to reconcile happens and there are signs of repentance and lasting change, pray for wisdom. Then move carefully in that direction, trusting God to protect and guide you both. What a testimony to this world of God's redemptive grace. I can only imagine how liberating that is for a couple who experiences the restorative power of forgiveness. It's a holy miracle that goes beyond any advice or wisdom of men.

If you are the one who caused the marriage to disintegrate, be patient. Pursue your former spouse with loving patience. Allow time to let your relationship heal with every date. Stay sexually pure and upright with her. Remember, she's like that rental car we talked about earlier. She is not your wife yet; she is your sister (1 Timothy 5:1–2).

Satan hates the holy institution of marriage. It's a threat to his dominion, and he will attack this fragile relationship. Yet our Heavenly Father is bigger. With the exception of your ex being an unbeliever, if there's an obvious redemptive process yoking you back together, explore it and protect it with diligence.

Blanket your courtship in prayer and a supportive community that believes in the miracle-working power of a loving God. When the Lord restores a marriage that's been ravaged, it's a wonderful opportunity to plan a celebration wedding with friends and family. Don't be afraid of baby steps. When the Lord is in it, our moving too slowly can't thwart his plans.

All of heaven is cheering for you, and so are your children.

CHECKING YOUR GAUGES

How long has it been since your divorce?

Do a Bible study on the topic of divorce. Is there biblical backing for remarriage in your situation?

What are your motives for pursuing another relationship?

STUDYING THE MAP

"Charm is deceptive, and beauty is fleeting; but a woman who fears the LORD is to be praised. Honor her for all that her hands have done, and let her works bring her praise at the city gate." Proverbs 31:30–31 NIV

REROUTING

It's important to be aware of what pushes our romantic buttons. Make a list of actions a lady friend might innocently do that turn you on romantically. Now make a list of actions you do that might defraud a woman.

Dating is an exclusive, intimate event between two people alone together, while courting is inclusive and involves a community; list the pros and cons of each.

REFUELING

Lord, I want you to be my one true love. Make me content with only you. Give me wisdom to know if you are calling me to singleness or marriage. Either way, help me treat all women like my sisters. There are times when I'm so lonely and desire the touch of a woman. Give me strength to remain celibate until I'm married. When I am weak, be my strength. Jesus, when you walked this earth, you were fully God and fully a man, so these feelings are not unfamiliar to you. Help me. Give me strength also to balance my fatherhood with any romantic pursuits. Only you can help me be a desirable man and still remain an attentive daddy. Thank you, Lord. Amen.

CHAPTER 15

A Two-Car Garage
(Remarriage)

"Hey! Who messed with my rearview mirror?"

As soon as I walked in, I wanted to leave. It was a singles' Christmas party at church. Many there were in college or barely out; I was in my midthirties. Greeting a few people, I scanned the room for a place to stand. I decided to stay just long enough to float in, make a few people laugh—that's my thing—and disappear when no one was looking.

Then I saw her. A woman, not a girl.

Golden hair fell across her shoulders. She glanced at me and continued talking to my friend Phillip.

He called from across the room, "Tez, I want you to meet someone."

After introducing me to Christine, he walked away. I made small talk for a few moments, but this woman was obviously way out of my league. Christine was different. She was mature, quiet, and refined.

Despite my insecurities, I decided to stay.

Throughout the evening when Christine chimed in to a conversation, it was worth listening. She intrigued me, but over the next few weeks I discovered how difficult it was to run into her at church. Apparently busy with a life outside the church singles group, she was hard to find. Finally we reconnected after a few weeks and became good pals. When the possibility of being more than friends eventually arose, I grew very cautious.

The Cuckoo's Nest

I was cautious with Christine for good reason. A few years earlier I had gotten involved with a beautiful woman who seemed very godly. After just a few weeks several things happened that let me know my character judgment was unreliable. First off, whenever she could, she would isolate us and initiate too much intimacy too soon. The desire for closeness can be so overwhelming. Then a man at church approached me, warning, "Be careful with that woman you're dating. I used to date her. She's trouble."

I took note and proceeded with caution. But it wasn't long before she revealed she had left her previous church because people were gossiping about her. I made another mental note but pressed on, thinking the best of her.

Then she told me she had received a prophecy about her future, and it included me.

"Really?" I waited for more.

"According to the prophecy, I'm supposed to go overseas and I won't be alone."

"So you're going with a team?"

"Well, no. I'm leaving for a short-term trip this summer. Don't you think you're supposed to join me?"

I tried to wrap my head around her insinuation: "Well, I don't feel called to that country and don't have the money anyway. But I'm excited for you."

"God can bring in your funds. I'm not worried about that. I'm just thinking it would make travel a lot easier on us if we were married."

"What? Wait. I'm still figuring out if you're . . . I mean, I don't even know your middle name. We just met three weeks ago."

Over the next few weeks she continued to push intimacy, marriage, and missions. I felt trapped and manipulated, but she made me feel desirable, and that was my Achilles' heel. Humorously enough, when she insisted on using my toothbrush one afternoon, that was the last straw. I decided to unshackle myself from this eccentric. Refusing to end the relationship, she asked when she could see me next. I had to be stern and it didn't end well, but I learned some valuable lessons. Never, ever allow a woman to move faster than I'm comfortable. And never date without others involved who can check in on us.

A few months later I heard she returned to an old boyfriend and was arrested for domestic abuse and possession of illegal drugs. Whew! Thank the Lord, he opened my eyes and rescued me when I lacked the discernment.

Needless to say I was fearful Christine might also be too good to be true. How could this incredible woman of God—who dedicated her entire adult life to missions—be thirty-six years old, beautiful, and never married? Did she have the heads of old boyfriends in the back of her freezer? After all, I had endured fatal attractions before and was happiest as a single. It had been several years since my divorce and I was recovering nicely. Living on my own was comfortable—financially and otherwise. I was finally gaining ground. I'd learned from trial and error that it's pretty hard to win the Indy 500 when you're towing crazy behind you. Things were brighter for me now, so why sabotage that?

Observing Christine for a year, nothing nutty popped up. Finally getting a clue that God might be saving this treasure for me, we mutually agreed to explore if God might be calling us to marry. So we spent the next few months seeking that answer through community-based courtship, which included our church friends, small group leaders, and pastor. It was refreshing to have other people involved rather than working out a major decision alone, the way I did with my first marriage.

This type of relationship isn't for everyone, especially if your church friends have no idea why they should be involved. Society tells us romantic relationships are a private affair, so unless you are blessed to have a community like ours, it's more likely a foreign concept for folks.

Once I realized the relationship was serious, I would try to include my kids in the process the best I could. At one point Sharaya even suggested that Christine would make a wonderful stepmother for her. But in the end, because they were not mature, I had to take even positive opinions from them with a grain of salt.

Finally, after a blessing from Christine's mother and eldest brother (her

father died when she was nine) our courtship ended in a helicopter above the Orlando amusement parks.

REMARRIAGE STATS
With 67% of second marriages also ending in divorce, it's unwise to throw caution to the wind.

Christine said yes and our engagement began. Six months later we exchanged vows. Then my bride turned and traded vows with my two children.

What followed was more like a celebration than a reception. We had a blast dancing with each other and the kids. But before we knew it, we found ourselves whisked away for a honeymoon. I had thirty seconds to say good-bye to Sharaya and Caleb. Suddenly I felt like I was abandoning them.

"I guess this is it, kids." My face revealed sadness and guilt.

"We love you, Dad. Have a great time." Sharaya hugged me.

"I'm terrible, sending you to a friend's home tonight so they can take you to the airport in the morning. I should be doing that."

"That's crazy." Caleb shook his head.

"I feel like I'm leaving you to fend for yourselves while I run off with my new wife."

Sharaya kissed me. "It's just a cruise—you'll be back."

Outside the church, I found Christine. Holding hands, we ran through a tunnel of lit sparklers and climbed into the antique car. The last thing I saw out the back window was my kids waving good-bye.

What just happened? Was I moving on without them? Would this be the day we began drifting apart? Would they ever care to visit me again?

Attempting to take my thoughts captive, I lifted my bride's hand and with a smile, kissed it. "Hello, Wife."

Adjustments

Christine and I had been married a week. After a magnificent honeymoon cruise around the Caribbean, we moved into her house. We entered the driveway and I pulled the vehicle into our Lilliputian, one-car garage, turned the motor off, and attempted to exit the automobile.

I couldn't get out. The car door hit the wall of the garage, so we both shut our doors and I backed out, attempting to park closer to the middle. Eventually I learned how to position the vehicle that allowed us both to exit the car. Of course Christine's automobile claimed the garage, leaving my car exposed to the elements. No problem, but where would I put a tool bench or lawn mower? Soon enough, the inside of the house also became cramped. Although we loved our little house, I knew we'd eventually need a bigger place if our family grew.

It did. Just six weeks after the wedding, we offered to take in my daughter.

Air Bags

"Toilet seat stays down, please," Christine reminded me.

"Who made that rule? I don't like having to lift it each time I use it."

"It's called being a gentleman." She grinned sweetly.

OK, so I'm human. After all, I'd been single for seven years. It took some adjusting. Even now I selfishly forget to accommodate my wife. But one thing about having your kids living with you (or even just visiting) is you learn as newlyweds that minor issues like toothpaste lids or toilet seats become small when you're trying to sync efforts as parents. Because my daughter was so accustomed to her biological mother and me disagreeing on everything, Christine and I learned to protect our marriage by presenting a united front. One of the greatest compliments Sharaya gave us occurred when she tried to play us against each other in order to get something she wanted:

"You guys are like one person. It's freaky."

Scoot Over

As a college guy in Central Florida I loved piling into a car on the weekends with six or seven other students and driving to the beach. We were cramped and had no air-conditioning, but we had a blast. I've lost some impulsiveness over the decades as my bottom has widened. If someone asks me to pile into a car with too many passengers, I offer alternatives. I don't scoot as readily as I used to.

Much like a crowded Ford Pinto, depending on your attitude and age, making room for others in your home can be uncomfortable or it can be fun. I suggest the fun.

Your child will go through some adjustments to your new wife. You can try to make the best of it—turn those discomforts into an adventure instead of a nuisance. But your real priority is to your new bride and best friend, so make the home hers right away. After all, she's the one who vowed to stay with you until death. Your kids didn't—and won't.

It's important to be sensitive to your child's needs when allowing your new spouse to claim her territory. However, in the end it's more about catering to your bride and your marriage. That's another good reason why remarrying too soon is a bad idea. Going into a new marriage before you or your child adjust to a broken home is just asking for complications.

Whatever the case, your child will have expectations about this new stepmom. Talking about those ahead of time will help tremendously. I can think of a dozen things that would have gone over better had my father just talked to me ahead of time. My stepmother wanted her home to be a certain way. Had issues been explained—like why I couldn't leave textbooks on the dining room table for days—transition would've been easier. Instead of feeling annoyed I could have better understood her need for tidiness. Communication is an amazing thing. I needed the reminder that Ethel was my dad's wife—his new life partner and the lady of the house. Besides, I was about to leave for college, so who was I to feel encroached upon?

I'm a firm believer that kids experience more security when they are aware of their place in the family as second to the spouse. Sure, some kids may show resentment; we all do when we don't get what we want. With a few exceptions, parents who display a tighter, exclusive relationship that doesn't include the offspring, by my observation, produce happier, well-adjusted children.

Many may not agree, but we need to model the priority of our new marriage. My kids needed to see that the woman with whom I exchanged vows is of highest importance. Granted, this is easier for the kids to swallow if it's their biological mother. Not so easy when it's a stepmom. Nevertheless, representing a solid marriage is still key. Part of that

SAY WHAT?

"I'm not saying to neglect the kids, but they won't exactly suffer by seeing their parents put each other at the top of the list . . . serving as relationship role models."
—Huffington Post blogger Jackie Morgan MacDougall, arguing that parents should prioritize their marriage[1]

model includes never allowing your son or daughter to come between you and your wife, causing division. The exception, of course, would be if you married an axe murderer.

Making little Suzie second can be a controversial idea. Especially if you're afraid she's going to tell Mommy, "Dad loves his new wife more than me."

Hollywood has shaped even the minds of Christians to believe it's selfish to put your marriage before your children. After all, those poor little kids need to be reassured that they are a parent's first priority, right?

Rubbish.

Kids come and go. They're born, you try to keep them from getting killed, disciple them the best you can, feed and clothe them, and then they move away. There's no lifetime vow exchanged. No promise to be there for them until death do you part. Look around. Do you see your kids initiating those vows with you? It might be time for a shift in thinking.

Ron L. Deal, National Director for Family Life Blended says it best:

It's a matter of significance. It's not that a spouse matters more than children, but rather that a strong marriage relationship contributes more significantly to the stability of the home than any other factor—including the children.

Your children will never suffer neglect because you make a

strong commitment to your new spouse. You don't have to choose between your spouse and your children; when you make your marriage your primary priority, you are actually choosing both. Placing your spouse in the "front seat" of your heart is good for your children, too. In fact, a healthy marriage means safety and protection for children.[2]

It may sound harsh, but showing the depth and commitment of your love for the Lord and then secondly for your wife is actually one of the kindest things you can model for your child.

Now guys, hear me, please. This doesn't apply to a mere girlfriend. If I'm putting a girlfriend before my kids, then I'm a jerk! I'm talking about prioritizing a wife. Apples and oranges.

Who Painted My Truck Pink?

Larry had been without a wife for a while. He worked full-time outside the home while raising his two children alone. Over time, the house became a mess. So he hired an organizer guru to come in and sort his house while he was away. Larry came home and couldn't find anything. Valuable items were thrown away, the worst loss being the keys to a safety deposit box, which required $150 to replace.

"What a disaster. It was tidy, but I was lost," says Larry.

Whether it's a well-meaning friend or a new wife, it's important to communicate what's important and what isn't when it comes to allowing them to change things. The sheets that are covering your window might be replaced with drapery—that's an improvement, a no-brainer. But what happens when your La-Z-Boy with a fridge in the armrest is moved to the curb? What if your bride's Siamese cat turns your daughter's bed into a litter box? You won't be able to foresee every problem, but eliminating some presumptions can be a great start.

When I married Christine I saw some décor that to me seemed unnecessary only to find it had memories tied to it from her pre-Tez days. I didn't care.

"What's this girly piece of mess?" I asked Christine, pulling it down from the cabinet.

"I got that when I lived in the Middle East. It's an authentic Turkish tea set."

"Ever used it?"

"Only once, but I love it. It's so pretty and my team and I used sets like this when we held meetings for students."

"Cool . . . so you've only used it once?"

Silence.

Setting it next to the other garage sale items I continued, "I mean, it doesn't really match anything, and there's no room to leave it setting out, right?"

"I suppose. It just reminds me . . ."

"You've got a new life now, Baby. Ready to move forward?"

"Um, yeah. I guess it's just clutter. Go ahead."

While downsizing can be healthy, I selfishly used my persuasive skills to barrel over Christine. I convinced her she was silly to keep something that I had absolutely no attachment to.

A few years later, I took a business trip to Turkey, every day drinking tea from almost identical cups like the ones we sold for a few bucks at the garage sale. I suddenly understood how an authentic tea set could hold so much meaning. Not having the chance to buy a replacement during my visit, I determined to purchase one next time. Since then, I've also met and become friends with the couple who gave the tea set to my wife. My heart still hurts for Christine's loss. Although I apologized, it remains a slight point of tension for us even today.

Justin went the second mile and bought an entirely new house in order to make sure his marriage started out on the right foot: "When we were engaged, my fiancée owned a home. Many people assumed I would simply move in. We felt it important to our marriage and our new family to have a common ground—a new home. That way we avoided any of the this-is-mine-that's-yours stuff. The new home automatically became ours. This isn't financially possible for every couple, but I would say if you can, do it. Moving into a new home bonded our family as one new unit. We realized eventually we even needed new flatware. For my bride, every time we used the old set, she saw herself sitting down to a meal with her ex. We were sometimes surprised by what household items mattered and what things didn't."

Men, when the new Mrs. moves in, make sure you communicate clearly what is important for you and the kids, but find out her expectations as well. Getting married later in life, Christine and I needed to learn that we had a history and friendships we didn't necessarily share, but were still very significant. Many of our possessions had memories and value attached to them which the other person had no clue about.

Saying Good-bye

Adding people to your family means new challenges. The new person's family ties, jobs, and other needs are sure to complicate your life. One of those issues may lead to the decision to move away to your new wife's hometown. What then? Whether you have custody of your child or not, there's a problem. You're either taking your child away from his or her mother, or you're moving away from your child. Thinking through all the potential things that may cause you to relocate is next to impossible. Not every scenario on your horizon will be obvious, just know these common issues:

1. If you and your bride hail from different cities, often the spouse with the most potential for career advancement will ask the new spouse to move there. Keep in mind that a job is different from a career. Careers often justify a move, while jobs are just something to pay the bills. Jobs come and go; careers are long term; know the difference.

2. Relatives play a part in where you live too. Talk all this through with your fiancée/bride. Your child has family too—on your ex-wife's side of the family. How will your relocation affect your child and their relatives?

3. Finally, the need for a new start in life can also lead to a relocation. For some, getting away from toxic relationships or cities that have bad memories associated with them may be what both of you need.

Thinking through ways to make the transition bearable for you and your child will make the journey a bit smoother.

Even though it's a blessing, a second marriage is always a complication for your family. There are adjustments, but if the Lord is in it, it will flourish and your child will be blessed by it. With the Lord at the center of your relationship, a small circle of believers to bounce decisions off, and your eyes a bit more open to what marriage should look like, it will survive.

CHECKING YOUR GAUGES

Read through the book of 1 Samuel. David could have opted for forbidden shortcuts to avoid prolonged difficulties and suffering under King Saul. How does David's example teach us delayed gratification as single men, when we long for a wife?

After studying all the Bible has to say about divorce and remarriage, do you feel released and free to remarry? Why or why not?

If marriage is an option, what are some ways you can prepare your child for the arrival of a stepmother? How can you prepare your house?

STUDYING THE MAP

"As iron sharpens iron, so one person sharpens another." Proverbs 27:17 (NIV)

REROUTING

Before the wedding, discuss with your fiancée if it's better to find a brand new place for the both of you. Talk about the differences between heirlooms and knickknacks.

If you have a daughter, what are some ways she has you wrapped around her finger? Think of ways this might lead to problems when your bride moves in. Make a list of ways you can prevent this.

If you have a son, what are you modeling for him about how males should treat the female gender? Do you need to make a list of habits you can help him unlearn?

REFUELING

Lord, I want to know beyond any doubt that it's OK to remarry before I even begin to date. Holy Spirit, help me know God's will for me. Protect me from pursuing the wrong woman and help me learn to wait for you to complete your healing in me. Reveal selfishness in me and transform my character, so I can expand my heart and life into a two-car garage. Give me wisdom on how best to prepare my child(ren) for a bonus mother. Help me make her #2 in my life after you, Father. In Christ's name, amen.

CHAPTER 16

Taking the Bus
(Blending Families)

"Don't make me stop this car!"

Once upon a time I was a school bus driver. At the start of each school year students would board my bus, stop for a moment, and check out the seating arrangements. They were trying to determine who was or wasn't safe to sit with. Eventually they got to know their fellow passengers, but each day things changed. Students didn't always sit in the same seats, so riders needed to be flexible and learn how to make the best of the situation. Sometimes new kids would begin riding, while others disappeared for several weeks if their parents drove them. Adjustments were constantly being made—some easy, others not so much. I observed a lot about habits and how stubborn people were when they wanted things to stay the same.

The community that happened inside that school bus was somewhat like blending a family. Transporting students and blending families both require assessment and coping skills when a new face is introduced to the mix. As a team, you and the new Mrs. must continually check that huge mirror above your driver's seat that helps you see what's going on and how to correct it when your passengers start acting squirrely with each other.

Don't Make Me Stop This Bus!

When I was a kid, my mom would often get aggravated at us four boys when we got too loud in the car. Some of her threats were funny but very effective. One in particular always shut me down.

Listen to FamilyLife Today radio interview, "The Myth of the Ideal Stepfamily."

"You need to quiet down before I kill us all. I mean it. I'll drive this car right into a tree if you boys don't hush!" The poor woman was probably on her last nerve.

When I began driving a bus-load of kids, I finally understood my mom's frustration. When the students got rambunctious, I could almost taste Mom's words on my tongue. Instead of threats, I would just pull over, turn off the bus, and stare at them in the mirror. They got it. It wouldn't take more than fifteen seconds to get them sitting down again and silenced.

Blending your family is going to produce some acting out at times. Attitudes of jealousy, irritation, and even anger can present themselves. The bus drivers of your family need to handle those issues and still get everyone home safely.

Christine's Initiation

When Christine and I got married, Christine already loved my children. They had spent plenty of time together prior to the wedding. But we had a hard first year of marriage when we allowed my teenage daughter to move in just a few weeks after the wedding. Sharaya had dropped out of school and had become a bit hard for her mother to handle. She asked if we could offer a safe place where Sharaya could start over fresh. After taking the time to count the cost, we agreed to move her in. We loved her so much and felt the Lord could give us the grace to help her succeed socially, academically, and spiritually.

Sharaya was a gem, putting up with the various rules and expectations we set in place. She agreed to everything we asked, but we knew how hard it was for her. We took away a lot of freedom she was used to having, and many times I required way too much from her, especially spiritually.

I wasn't satisfied with how slow God was working and often tried to take over for him by pointing out sin in my daughter's life. That usually went over like a Baby Ruth bar in a swimming pool. On top of that, working as a sergeant at a maximum security prison, I often came home and treated Sharaya like an inmate, barking orders and demanding no questions.

Christine, on the other hand, had a bit more compassion for Sharaya, and she often helped me see I was being too harsh. It seems I apologized daily for something I did to break Sharaya's spirit. My wife poured all she had into helping Sharaya thrive as a homeschooled child. She even took a month-long work sabbatical in order to jump-start our daughter's academic excellence.

It helped a bit. We saw Sharaya excel in many areas of her life, but much of her outward change was only to appease us. Sadly, like many kids of divorce, Sharaya had an eject button installed on her bus seat. This allowed her to return to her mother and her former life before we had time to address some of her heart issues. Suddenly our daughter was gone, leaving Christine and me feeling confused.

Dads, don't be discouraged if your story seems similar. Situations can be out of our control, but our hope is placed in trusting God's sovereignty. As parents we can choose to second-guess our wisdom or we can relax in the knowledge that nothing catches God off guard. He allows us to have seasons where we can influence our children for long periods and short. Whether we have full custody or just visits, we learn to trust the Lord and his will, no matter the outcome.

A few years later when Sharaya reached adulthood, she apologized and thanked us for all we did to help her. She acknowledged all the love and sacrifice shown her and recalled some pretty happy moments with us, some of her favorite memories being those with Christine.

Today my firstborn is married to a wonderful man named David. I enjoy my visits with Sharaya. We can talk about anything together, and we laugh a lot—we get each other. She's had a lot of hardships in life, and I'm proud of who she is becoming. Those times when she lived with me are treasured moments.

Speed Bumps

Changes happen when you mix households. Your friends may not fully appreciate how your family size has changed. Others (especially relatives) may

RESOURCES FOR BLENDED FAMILIES
Find hundreds of resources for blended families at
www.familylife.com

not know how to react to your new family. You know those blinking red stop signs that pop out on the side of a school bus? It can feel like you have one of those attached to your blended home.

Sarah Kinbar has this advice in her article "Blended Families":

> Get out and socialize with other families. Many blended family parents find that some friends are not willing to embrace a big change in family structure. The friends we're most drawn to can connect with all of our children. Since we've blended, we've made new friends or stayed connected with old friends who have big hearts and have welcomed the whole gang.[1]

You probably lost friends with the divorce, so this won't be new territory for you. The great thing is you also met new friends who will embrace your blended family, just like those who embraced you as a single-again dad.

Those speed bumps can be obnoxious, even painful if you're driving too fast. Slowing down a bit as your family learns to blend helps lessen the impact of those bumps.

There's so many different dynamics going on simultaneously, it can be tough to know which relationship to tackle first; the stepparents, stepkids, stepsiblings, half-siblings, and more. The list is extensive. Rather than attempt the impossible task of addressing every possible relationship, perhaps it's best to blanket the entire topic biblically.

Bottom Line

I enjoy watching old *Brady Bunch* episodes. That blended family always looked so happy no matter the problem. We never observe much to worry about with the Bradys. In their first television episode, which aired in 1969, we see a backyard wedding followed by a honeymoon that includes all six kids and Alice the maid. Not my idea of a beautiful consummation, but whatever. By episode three, everyone appears to have completely adjusted to the family's population explosion, and all is well for the next five seasons. If only it were that way in real life. Perhaps that's why they canceled the show decades ago. The sitcom *Modern Family* is more like real life these days. The fact is, if you decide to remarry, life is going to get a lot more complicated than Hollywood reveals. However, if the Lord has ordained this relationship, you can move in the confidence of knowing that he's walking all of you through it.

Unlike Mike or Carol Brady, dying to self and putting others above my own desires is difficult for me. I can be very selfish. Yet I know I can't begin to teach this to my family if I don't first model it.

My wife, Christine, has great advice for couples trying to blend a family:

> Be sensitive, patient, and understanding with the kids. Listen to them. They didn't choose to blend this family. They didn't have a choice—so just knowing you're listening goes a long way.

We all have to die to self. Although you still hold your kids to the high standard of loving the new family and dying to self, you must be patient. They are young, and not always prepared to embrace mature responses to challenges like this.

R.E.S.P.E.C.T.

You and the Mrs. might need some time getting used to a stepchild. More than likely you'll be compelled to feel accepted by your new son or daughter by being a buddy. I'm not convinced we're ever supposed to be a buddy to children (whether ours or someone else's). Adults are meant to be authority figures. It's true our relationship changes when our kids reach adulthood—from protector to advisor. But for minors who need mentoring, direction, and guidance, I believe it's a mistake to chum up and try to win over a child's affections. Men, if you see your new wife trying too hard to be a buddy, as her protec-

READ MORE ABOUT RESPECT FOR STEPPARENTS

tor it's your job to give gentle reminders to her and the kids that she's running the home along with you.

Call me old fashioned, but respect doesn't have to be earned. Although it's nice to earn it, some titles are given with the understanding that respect comes with it. The title of Father or Mother (biological or otherwise) comes with a built-in honor element. Assuming the adult isn't abusive, respect for any adult family member should be reinforced by Dad and Mom if we notice the contrary.

Our own little Cindy or Bobby may not receive it well, but we should keep things in perspective. Our children are immature and often don't fully understand respect until they have kids of their own. Our wife's success at a seamless transition into "bonus mom" is highly dependent on us dads. She needs us to help catch her up. Taking the time to inform her about each child's personality helps her know how to approach each unique child when it comes to misunderstandings or conflict.

Your wife needs to know you will step in and play the bad guy so she doesn't have to. That also works the other way around if she brings her own kids into the mix. In order to help you succeed as the new man of the house, gently ask her to step in if her kids disobey or ignore your requests.

How to Be the Bonus Dad

It's natural for you or your wife to fall into various roles in order to counteract the other. If she's the disciplinarian with her child, you might feel the need to be lenient or vice versa. Don't fall into either mode arbitrarily, but discuss this with your spouse so you both can be intentional and strategic about your roles.

Guys seem to have a bit harder time as stepparents. With so many bad stepdads on the local news and in movies, you can feel like you're getting a bad rap. The public almost expects you to be a jerk that doesn't care for the welfare of another man's biological child. It's discrimination and the assumption isn't fair, but it's common. It can drive you to walk on eggshells and become resentful.

You more than likely already know you can never replace their real father. But you have the splendid opportunity to bless your family by living above reproach as the extra father. So what does living above reproach look like? It's different for each family and includes a whole lot of suggestions from the biological parent. Talk with your wife and the child about what they consider to be appropriate touching, verbal sentiments, or clothing around the house. Then share what you consider to be appropriate.

This isn't a one-time discussion either. As the child matures the rules may change, and if you are not aware of those changes, it can place you in a very uncomfortable situation. Allowing a two-year-old stepdaughter to run through the house in her pajamas is one thing. What about when she's twelve? Allow no ammunition for anyone to say you're unworthy of living in the same house with these stepchildren. Show the world you're qualified by drawing out your new wife with questions. Be a student of each stepchild's history and character. This could be your chance to be a hero.

I have a good friend, Jono, whom I admire as a shining example of this. He married our friend Jen and became an instant parent. Over the years Jono has become a wonderful dad to his stepdaughter who respects and loves him. She calls him Dad and the interactions between them are like any other father and child. There's never a hint of hesitation when it comes to either physical touch or rebukes. It's difficult to remember Jen's daughter is not also Jono's.

He takes his care to another level. He even protects Jen from any undesired stress by doing all the verbal interactions and visitation planning with the biological father. Cooperation takes place regarding house rules, curfews, report cards, school projects, and social calendars. With everyone on the same page, potential irritations between the two households are alleviated. This communication between the two dads ensures the mother and child (now a teen) feel loved and looked after.

Putting a Baby in the Blender

Having a baby together can also bring surprises. When Christine and I decided to have children we assumed my kids would be involved in the lives of our babies. Sharaya and Caleb embraced the blessing of having little sisters, but with the huge age difference, bonding was slower than I imagined. My kids were teens by then with their own sets of friends. They had grown accustomed to life without little sisters.

My two youngest girls developed a small bit of history with Caleb because he lived with us for a while and became close to his baby sisters. But their relationship with Sharaya (who can't visit as often) tends to be more like a relationship between cousins. There's nothing wrong with that; it's just life. When lifestyles, distance, or generational gaps sculpt relationships, be prepared to release your dreamy expectations of a close-knit family. Sometimes your Brady Bunch is not going to happen. You're still a family.

Back in my bus driving days, when I saw trouble brewing, my first defense in helping make peace between agitated students was to create seat assignments and get them talking to each other.

There were times I saw some jealousy rise between my blended offspring. Because I had become more laid back, sometimes Caleb would mention how his baby sisters got away with more than he did. With the gap between my first two kids and my last two, my oldest were teens by the time Christine and I started our family. I had mellowed a lot since my early twenties, so I raised my second batch very differently. I tried to take time to draw out my older children on how they felt when they observed how I provided for the girls, disciplined them, or treated them. They seemed to understand that being older changed my parenting skills. But

"It's no use to preach to children if you don't act decently yourself."
—Theodore Roosevelt
(1858–1919)[2]

there was so much more at play—spiritual growth, career and income changes, and the synergy that comes from raising children with the mother in the home. I'm not sure if even today Sharaya and Caleb fully comprehend why these changes affected my parenting style. That's OK; they're sharp adults, and I'm confident one day they'll appreciate the difference.

Similar to misunderstandings among students on a bus, addressing an annoyance usually seemed to help. I'm a bit of a confronter because I believe it's the unspoken irritations that cause the most dissention. Talking about it makes the issue seem smaller and solvable. Without discussion, the issues can reach epic magnitude.

Speak often of forgiveness toward one another and create the habit of erasing small accounts. Refusing to harbor tiny offenses keeps them from building up. So when possible, apply Ephesians 4:32 which says, "Be kind to one another, tenderhearted, forgiving one another, as God in Christ forgave you."

In the middle of all the refereeing it's important to remind yourself what it's all about. Blending families complicates your life. In fact, many say the phrase "blended family" is deceiving because it makes it sound so smooth. Perhaps "mingled family" is more accurate. Either way, we have an added element that helps—the Lord. With his help anything is possible. Keeping your focus clear will help tremendously. It can be easy to feel overwhelmed and hopeless. Don't give up. Be patient. Everyone needs time to get used to each other. Family has a way of rubbing you the wrong way sometimes. Some of your worst character traits are going to bubble to the top, exposing your need to repent and pray for a changed heart. Leading this new household isn't always about making you happy. Sometimes it's just making you holy.

No Shortcuts

I enjoyed driving a school bus. I liked the variety—never knowing what each day held. Would there be a fight on the bus? Would I get the coveted field trip assignment? Maybe I'd get the preschool run with all the cute little ankle-biters, each one strapped into a restraint seat. I looked forward to a new adventure every morning. There's only one day I remember hating my job.

I had just picked up a load of kids from the school when the dispatcher advised me I needed to return and get a student who had missed the bus. I was on the highway, and there was no exit in which I might turn around for another five miles.

I was young and stupid, and I made a very, very bad choice that day. You know those unpaved spots on the freeway median where cops often park? I decided to take a short cut by making an illegal U-turn across one of those.

In a school bus.

Filled with children.

When I turned there was a slight dip in the median and the back bumper of that long yellow bus couldn't clear it. The ground reached up and grabbed the bumper making it impossible to move. I was stuck.

In a school bus.

Filled with children!

The dispatcher sent another bus to take the kids home. Once the tow truck pulled me out, I was sent home, suspended for four weeks without pay. Humiliated and embarrassed, I strolled the walk of shame to my car, talking to myself.

"What kind of nut are you, Tez? You don't take risks with other people's children. It could have ended very badly had God not protected you from your idiocy."

I learned an expensive lesson that day. Don't take shortcuts. It's not worth it. You can say the same for blending two family units together. Take your time. Don't try to create your own private exit ramps when you're feeling overwhelmed.

Patience is underrated. Think of how long it took to get used to your own child when he or she first entered your world. We underestimate the amount of time it takes to adjust to new family members—biological, adopted, or blended. Slow down your expectations and pray for your little family and wait for the Lord to change their hearts—and yours.

CHECKING YOUR GAUGES

What expectations do you have regarding your blended family?

To what length have you talked with your kids about their own expectations?

In what areas do you foresee potential speed bumps? What's your plan?

STUDYING THE MAP

"So whatever you wish that others would do to you, do also to them, for this is the Law and the Prophets." Matthew 7:12

REROUTING

Have a discussion with your wife about each child (hers and yours). Discuss their history, personality traits, quirks, habits, and hobbies. Make a list of ways you can both engage with each child and slowly integrate into their world.

Go to 5lovelanguages.com to take the free online test for each family member and discuss the results among yourselves.

Set aside a family day at least twice a month when everyone can be together for game night or pizza and a movie. Plan a family vacation. Although more expensive, it should include everyone—even those children who live elsewhere. Making a new history can only happen when you spend time together.

REFUELING ───────────────────────────────────

Father, you have bound us together as a family, but sometimes all I see is a failure to blend. I know you saw this coming, and it's no surprise to you we are all living in the same house. Thank you for trusting all of us with this gift. I screw up sometimes, so help me to speak words of love and respect even when I'm correcting the children. As the head of this new family, I need wisdom above my own experience so I can help my family glorify you. In our brokenness, let us be examples of your grace and restoration, a light on a hill, so unbelievers can see the Holy Spirit in us and be drawn to Jesus. When conflicts arise, give us forgiving hearts and unfailing love for one another. In Jesus's name I ask all these things. Amen.

PART 3

Caution: Men at Work

The Less Familiar Route
(Abiding in Christ with Your Kids)

Honk honk. *"Watch where you're going, idiot!"*

In his famous poem "The Road Not Taken," Robert Frost wrote about deciding to take a route "less traveled" and how that choice changed his life. As single dads we too face a decision. We can stay in the car and keep going. It's a good road and it will get us places. Or we can get out of the vehicle and stroll down that other pathway. I meet men all the time who have ignored the less familiar road, preferring the comfort of the ruts made from previous travelers. For me, that rut is the well-worn road of activity and good works. It's an ongoing challenge to be still, to be his child. The lesser-worn road is one I need desperately to take. Can I suggest you turn off your engine, step out of the car, and come with me? Let's discover together something we might be missing.

Modeling our walk with God openly for our kids is good. Not only do they need to observe us praying, reading the Bible, and giving tithes, they also need to see our love for God in our attitudes at home. Not as a show. Matthew 6 warns that our motives need to be pure. Deuteronomy tells us to instruct our children in the ways of the Lord. So I often unpack spiritual conversations strategically while walking or driving with the kids.

All this is good. Ephesians 6:4 says that we are to bring our children up in the "discipline and instruction of the Lord." This is most effective when we learn to simply be a Christian in front of them. Talking about what it means to be a Christian is great, but even more effective is to let them see what the Christian life looks like when you live that out in the midst of trials or pain.

"And these words that I command you today shall be on your heart. You shall teach them diligently to your children, and shall talk of them when you sit in your house, and when you walk by the way, and when you lie down, and when you rise."
—Deuteronomy 6:6–7

How do we do that? Most of this book, after all, is full of suggestions on stepping up your game—acting upon something or doing good works. So are we to neglect relaxing in the Lord's presence? Of course not. There are times to be a Mary and times to be a Martha. It's on the road less taken where we dads stop trying to impress others by being on top of things and instead sit at Christ's feet.

Sit or Spin

Now I know the story of Mary and Martha isn't the most manly story for this book, but it's the best passage to make my point. In Luke 10, Jesus arrived at Mary and Martha's house about mealtime. As the perfect hostess, it was Martha who let him in. Notice the details. Martha's sister, Mary, sat at Jesus's feet and heard his words, but Martha was distracted with serving. She said, "Lord, do you not care that my sister has left me to serve alone? Tell her then to help me" (v. 40).

Jesus basically answered, "Martha, chill out."

When I read this, I wince. I really connect with God when I'm serving him. It feels good, and I often feel his pleasure. So where does that leave me? What did Mary have that Martha needed? What was the "good portion" (v. 42) Mary chose? In a world filled with distractions, the story of Mary and Martha can frustrate us guys who are prone to *do* rather than stop and become.

The Gospels are clear that Jesus felt pretty comfortable in the home of Mary and Martha and their brother, Lazarus. The four weren't just acquaintances; they were close friends. The siblings spoke to Jesus as if he were family. He was at ease with them.

If you read no further, you could assume Mary was a bit lazy. But John's account of that same visit (chap. 12) gives us more detail. Mary took a pound of very costly oil and anointed Jesus's feet, then wiped it up with her hair. The whole house was filled with the fragrance.

Obviously Mary was so dedicated to Jesus that no expense was too great or demanding. This attitude is the kind of approach God desires from us. It's illuminating to contrast the two siblings' relationship. Martha was so comfortable with Jesus that she openly included him in her frustration. "Don't you care?" she asked.

Humorously, Martha didn't *suggest* that he ask Mary to help; she told him directly. Jesus responded tenderly: "Martha, Martha, you are anxious and troubled about many things, but one thing is necessary. Mary has chosen the good portion, which will not be taken away from her" (Luke 10:41–42).

If you're like me, you have to make a choice as a dad to stop trying to be the best. While it's true that a lot of men need to step it up in the area of fatherhood, I can err in the other direction too—thinking excellent parenting is something we do to please God. But we must seek the good part, like Mary. In Matthew 6:33, Jesus tells us our highest priority in life should be to seek the kingdom of God and his righteousness.

You might ask, what did Jesus mean when he spoke of that good part that he wouldn't take away from Mary?

The apostle John might have the easiest answer: "For all that is in the world—the desires of the flesh and the desires of the eyes and pride of life—is not from the Father but is from the world. And the world is passing away along with its desires, but whoever does the will of God abides forever" (1 John 2:16–17).

Let me reword that for us fathers.

Everything the world throws at single dads—lust for sexual encounters, desire for possessions for ourselves and our kids, recognition as good dads—it all comes from mere humans. There's nothing honorable or long-lasting about it, because this planet is fizzling out, along with all the stuff in it. But fathers who choose the good portion (that of spending time in God's presence) have chosen something that lasts forever.

We can work harder than a chiropractor at a rodeo trying to do the right thing as Christian dads. Yet the moments with God that we accumulate in this life will be ours forever, never taken away from us. Like Mary, we must learn to be *in* Christ. So what does that look like? Galatians 5:22–23 lists a bunch of characteristics or fruits that take us away from the ruts and toward that unused path. A path that gets so overgrown in places we have to wield our spiritual machete to get to those fruits. Let's take a look at those.

Love

The first fruit mentioned in Galatians 5 is love. I have to love not only my family and friends, but strangers too. It doesn't stop there. I must love even my enemies. It really doesn't matter if I travel the world as a missionary and teach myself a dozen languages; if I can't love others like Christ does, then I'm just making noise. I might as well be singing "What Does the Fox Say?"

I can be a student of sound doctrine and spend my life becoming an excellent theologian, able to defend the faith against the most aggressive atheists and lead thousands to Christ. I might be able to move in the power of all the gifts and attend every Holy Ghost Prophetic Conference. I might even have enough faith to pull people right out of their wheelchairs. Still, if I can't love, I'm a big zero.

I could give away all my cash, my car, my house, or even die for the Lord as a martyr . . . OK, you get the point. Those would all be wonderfully good deeds, but if I never learned to love, it's all in vain. I'd say Paul was pretty clear about where God places love on his list of priorities. You might have astounding faith that makes one's jaw drop. You might have hope on steroids. But 1 Corinthians 13 says being a loving person is better than any of those. Ask the Lord to teach you to love.

Joy

I believe joy is vastly different from deep happiness. Happiness can easily change with our circumstances. Joy, however, comes from spending time in God's presence. (There's that nod to Mary again.) So maybe it's more accurate to call it "the joy of the Lord."

When we fully understand how hopelessly dead we were, how desperately we needed a Savior, and what Christ did for us—joy can bubble up and drive us to worship.

I find I'm most joyful when I'm gripped by the fact that I was dead and perilously close to hell when Jesus snatched me up. In those moments I can't *do* anything. I just want to sit still and *be* the rescued one. I need to better learn what real joy is.

Peace

I used to know a woman who had a habit of creating crises in her life. It seemed she was addicted to turmoil. I'm not sure if it made her feel more alive or if she merely enjoyed the attention, but every crisis that came upon her was self-inflicted. It was always something—an unexpected non-sufficient funds charge from her bank, a pending eviction, or an embarrassing car repossession. She never seemed to see it as her fault because she felt she was the victim. Her world was never in a state of peace very long, and it was sad to watch.

Isaiah 26:3 reminds us that our Master will keep us in perfect peace if our minds are steadied on him. It's easy in the early years of a divorce to lose tranquility when you've embraced the fragile peace of this world. A lot of doo-doo hits you. If the peace of Christ isn't your soap of choice, then even a really good fire hose won't help.

It's no secret that Christians struggle with peace. Even the disciples who hung out all the time with Jesus wrestled with this. In Matthew 14, Jesus had just finished feeding thousands of people with one boy's lunch. They saw the miracle—they were part of it. Yet only a few hours later on a stormy sea, they were freaking out, thinking they were going to die.

This wasn't a single incident. The need for reassurance was an ongoing essential for them. Even after he died, Jesus reminded the frightened followers to rest in his peace. They were likely thinking they might be next to die at the hands of the Romans. Then Christ appears and comforts them with a greeting of peace. In fact, John 20 shows us three times in just a few days where Jesus needs to give this blessing to the fearful disciples. He knew that they would go through tribulations, but He wanted them to "take heart" because he had "overcome the world" (John 16:33).

Scripture makes it clear: peace is a gift. Yet I so often try to obtain it on my own. Dads, you can't *do* peace. You can only *be* peaceful. So don't be anxious about stuff but lift up your requests to the Lord with thanks. Then the peace of God that goes way beyond your comprehension will protect you against worry (adapted from Phil. 4:6–7). Ask the Lord for real peace.

Patience

Whether you're waiting on traffic lights or the fulfillment of dreams, you still have to wait. No one is born with patience—just look at newborn babies. They have zero tolerance for hunger and discomfort.

I can be a big baby too. I want instant everything, especially with my kids. Perhaps you share my frustration. Just trying to get your little ones out the door in the morning can be a test. Shoes can't be found, hair won't get combed, lunches are forgotten. If patience isn't already in us, it's going to show, and it won't be pretty. Yet even in the midst of these annoyances, the Lord can mature us.

We need to understand, impatience is about not trusting God. For me, embracing that fact was like trying to insert contact lenses while on a roller coaster. It took me a long time to finally get it right. I just couldn't seem to understand how impatience had anything to do with a short-coming in me. Wasn't it about other people or things slowing me down? After all, I wouldn't be so impatient if it weren't for things like my outdated mobile device hindering my efficiency.

My problem was I didn't think God was doing a good job at planning my day. I didn't trust his sovereignty and control. But the Lord in his mercy finally helped me connect the dots and repent.

While most of our irritations are minor and short-lived, some can stretch over months or years. It can be tremendously significant when it involves illness, financial trouble, or a strained relationship. Being at the feet of Jesus during these times can fix much more than if we're hanging in the kitchen with Martha trying to do something productive. In desperation we might give God deadlines, but he rarely works on our timeline. One sign of spiritual maturity is the ability to calmly abide during the stress of temporary irritations or prolonged hardship. It's a great testimony of your trust in the Lord and teaches your kids the same as they watch your response.

Kindness

The world might say that if you're kind to nice people, then you must be full of kindness. But the Sermon on the Mount is pretty clear that Christians are expected to live at a higher standard—being kind to all people, even the evil ones. I've heard it said that hurt people *hurt* people. Similar to a dog that has been abused, they can lunge out and bite. Still, I'm expected to return that with kindness? Fail.

Acts of kindness are one thing; being kind is another. We could knock ourself out with kind deeds and get caught up in good works again. It's a good thing, but *doing* kind deeds all day will eventually wear us out. We'll come to the end of all we can give when we try to make kindness solely about doing. If we truly want to *be* kind, here's what that looks like.

Kindness is saying a tender word of love and encouragement to another. It's even being tender with a rebuke. Kindness is a soft touch or a smile. It's mirroring the love of God. It's thinking the best of others and giving folks grace when they offend or make mistakes. Kindness can be done without ever getting up out of your chair. And I believe it begins with family.

Sadly, kindness is often forgotten when dealing with our relatives. Ironically and tragically, many people display their most unkind behavior with the ones they should love the most. That's hypocrisy and I'm guilty of it.

I pray for kindness and gentleness so my girls can feel the heart of God touching them with each word I speak and each time I hold their hand. As a man I can be so rough without meaning to. Will you do me a favor? Pray for God to soften my approach. I'm already praying for you.

Goodness

Goodness and kindness are twin fruits—almost interchangeable. The Bible says every good and perfect gift comes from the Father above. Philippians 4 tells us anything that is noble, lovely and right, pure, excellent and worthy of respect—these are all good things to focus on. It seems from my experience, when my mind is focused on good things, it shows on the outside. People can most see what we're made of by what comes to the surface during times of stress. If in the midst of turmoil goodness comes out, it will point people to God—the source of all good.

What does goodness look like? How does it show itself in our lives? If you take all the other fruits addressed in this chapter and put them in a box, you could label that box "Goodness." Being a good man, a good father, means flowing back and forth among these character traits of God.

A good man is kind, peaceful, gentle, faithful, joyful, and more. Of course we're going to screw up. But we can still be good men—full of goodness.

The difference between goodness and kindness is this. I can spank my child or testify against a guilty murderer—and I'm still good. What makes me kind is if I comfort my child after a spanking or refuse to gossip about the convicted murderer.

Jesus was *good* when he turned over the tables of the money-changers in the temple. He was *kind* when he healed the blind man. All of this is summed up in the word *love*. Love is both kind and good, always seeking to minister to the needs of others.

Being good doesn't always mean we are nonthreatening. For example, courage is good, but it's not always risk-free. In C. S. Lewis's *The Lion, the Witch and the Wardrobe* Aslan is described as not necessarily being safe, but always good. The Bible too is full of men who were both good and dangerous: Noah, Abraham, Moses, Joshua, David, Peter, Paul, and others. I desire to be filled with goodness like that.

"Just because you're a man doesn't mean that you can't raise your kid. I think that families should stay together, but if you are a single father, don't give up no matter what they say."
—actor Nicolas Cage[1]

Faithfulness

Songs about God's faithfulness have always choked me up. I guess it's the fact that he remains so committed to me even though I so often fail to reciprocate. Although I love him, my heart is prone to wander. Fortunately he has me on a short leash. I never seem to travel far from him before he yanks me to his side again. I'm so grateful for that.

I can't count how many times as a teen and young adult I fell down at the feet of Jesus and repented. He was there every time, and still is—faithful and true. My Redeemer never refused entry back into the throne room and into his arms. I was never on probation—although I often acted like it. He is always faithful, always committed to communion with me. Perhaps that's why I have never left the faith since choosing to follow him at the age of six. His loyalty to me over the years continues to win my heart.

The Lord and I have been together almost half a century. These days I choose to sit a bit closer to my Savior. But although my body may be quieter, my mind still likes to sneak a walkabout. I suppose that's part of the fall. I look forward to that day when I will be set free from this rot known as *the flesh* and be like Christ forever.

That being said, are we capable of faithfulness apart from heaven? Can we in this fallen world ever truly be faithful? Sure. I don't think faithfulness is about being sinless, which is impossible. It's about living a lifestyle of repentance and finishing the race. Being faithful to the end.

Maybe faithfulness is best explained by sketching out what a nonfaithful individual looks like. Unfaithfulness shows itself in one who chooses extended periods of time running away from the Lord, pursuing the world's pleasures. They are in and out of church fellowship. An unfaithful person rarely talks about the Lord unless there's a crisis or a religious holiday. His kids might be sent to church or dropped off. But with Dad not involved himself, they don't fully learn what it's like to be part of a church community.

When we reduce Christianity to merely the religious hobby of attending church, we do our kids such a disservice. I want to show my kids that walking with the Lord is a lifestyle, not an activity. Activities, much like the Boy Scouts, can be outgrown. If we demonstrate Christianity as simply another optional activity, then for our children to attend church as adults might seem childish to them. So if we haven't been faithful to God, our youngster grows up having no idea why he needs God consistently. Instead he learns to place God on a shelf like a magic genie, until a crisis comes along.

A man faithful to God has a life that is so entwined with his Maker that he cannot see a separation possible between the two. When we are loyal, our entire worldview includes a God element. Every decision we make, action we take, daily conversation—everything is mingled in with our Creator's DNA.

Be faithful. To the end.

Gentleness

The New Testament has two similar references regarding being a gentle father. One is in Ephesians 6:4, instructing dads not to provoke their children to anger. The other is Colossians 3:21, again telling us not to discourage our kids by being too harsh. That says a lot about the nature of men. If God's Word is telling us twice to lighten up, obviously we must by default lean toward harshness.

Christine has to remind me at times to ease up a bit when I expect my children to be smarter, wiser, more alert, or more spiritually mature. I tend to push and push, forgetting the hugs. If I'm not careful with their sensitive and tender hearts, my words can come across cruel and calloused, making our home an unsafe place for them to be transparent.

Asking the Holy Spirit to make me gentle is something I continually pray for. I don't know my own strength when it comes to handling my little girls. But it goes beyond the physical. Equally vital is treating others' hearts with gentleness, using tender words.

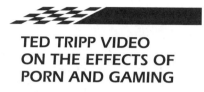

TED TRIPP VIDEO ON THE EFFECTS OF PORN AND GAMING

Self-Control

This last fruit almost seems to lean more toward good works than faith. To control myself feels so much like work; it's hard to embrace it as something that is part of my new identity. Denying myself something just feels like I'm reverting back to a good deed.

Of course it's not just about saying no to something. It's about saying no by faith. Denying myself is work, of which I get the glory. But saying no by faith gives God the glory because in this case I'm bringing nothing to the table. No good works. When I exercise self-control by faith, then I'm just abiding or "being" and Christ gets the glory.

I lack self-control most when I'm trying to fast. I've done long-term fasting with no problem. It's those one-day fasts that kill me. I love my wife's cooking. My flesh is so weak that I almost always break the fast by early evening.

Let's talk about something other than fasting, lest you think I'm trying to come off super-spiritual. What about pornography, the male ego, or punishing my child in anger? All of these attempt to pry their way into my world and ruin me. I have found that trying to overcome sin on my own is pretty ineffective. It always ends up with me on the floor in repentance. Only when I release control and admit that my own righteousness is a joke can God be glorified. His righteousness is my only hope.

I know the word is *self-controlled*, but that's a misnomer really. As soon as I let *self* in there, I'm in trouble. It might be better described as

Christ-controlled, for it's only with him that I can succeed in growing this fruit of the Spirit.

All these fruits can feel at times like they are good works produced solely by you. First of all, let's not kid ourselves; anything good in us only comes from the Father. We can't dredge up these character traits on our own. That's why they are called *fruits of the Spirit* instead of *fruits of [insert your name here]*. Our fruits are all mushy bananas covered in fuzzy mold. Nobody wants them. We can't even make muffins with them.

It's true we can stir up certain habits on our own. This may change our actions but not our character. In other words, if I'm not gifted in being kind, I might consciously attempt to do kind deeds to others until it becomes only an ingrained habit. That's all well and good. But I'm not capable of keeping that up. At some point God needs to take over in order for transformation to happen, otherwise I'm defaulting back to good works.

Here's the secret. We have to die to ourselves. Jesus said unless a seed falls to the ground and dies it can't bear fruit. Our innate human nature must be replaced by God's nature. On our own, we can't do anything to make this happen. It can only burst forth with the gift of his Spirit dwelling in us and the wonderful fruit he distributes to his children.

There's a time for you as a single dad to be driving down the road toward your destination. There's also a time to get out, stretch your legs, and walk the road that is so often ignored. Along that road are fruit trees filled with love, joy, peace, patience, kindness, goodness, faithfulness, gentleness, and self-control.

My advice: eat more fruit.

CHECKING YOUR GAUGES ——————————————

In what ways do you enjoy serving God? How do you best connect with
   him?

Are you more prone to take the busy road (Martha) or the road less taken (Mary)? Why is that?

List which fruits of the Spirit are most obvious in your life. Which fruits are scrawny and need attention?

STUDYING THE MAP

"Do not lay up for yourselves treasures on earth, where moth and rust destroy and where thieves break in and steal, but lay up for yourselves treasures in heaven, where neither moth nor rust destroys and where thieves do not break in and steal. For where your treasure is, there your heart will be also." Matthew 6:19–21

REROUTING

Schedule a retreat for yourself where you can get away and hear from the Lord.

Don't take work or a computer with you. Take time to be silent before the Lord and listen to him. Do not pray. Do not ponder how you can do better in some area of your life. Just spend time being his child. Spend the time writing what he's shown you during the retreat.

REFUELING

Lord, I've been doing things for so long I've forgotten how to be. Teach me, Father, how to rest in your presence like Mary. I know the importance of stepping up to be a better dad, but what I want more is to be full of you. I want your Holy Spirit in me so much there's no room for anything else. Fill me with your fruits, God. Transform me into a mighty man of God. Amen.

Recalling Your Destination
(The Big Picture)

"Are we there yet?"

By now you might be either overwhelmed by all the things this book says you must be on top of—or excited you now have a list of responsibilities you can accomplish so you can feel good about yourself again.

Neither of those are my intent for you. I don't want you to close this book feeling discouraged—nor do I want you to feel you can be Super Dad by bringing some form of good deeds to the table. Pride, performance, and self-reliance will always be your Kryptonite.

What I'm praying for is that you will feel the weight of single fatherhood lifted by the grace of God, the final work of Christ's blood on the cross, and the power of the Holy Spirit working in and through you. My hope is that you'll walk away from these pages humbled, knowing you can probably improve in some areas. But I also hope you'll be encouraged, knowing there's nothing you can't do when Jesus is on the throne of your heart. "It is the LORD who goes before you. He will be with you; he will not leave you or forsake you. Do not fear or be dismayed" (Deut. 31:8).

During interviews, singer/songwriter Amy Grant has alluded a few times that life is messy. She ought to know. She has survived a controversial and highly publicized divorce. Even after widespread criticism and losing a huge fan base, she continues to recognize God's grace in the midst of a broken world. Despite ruined relationships, destroyed homes, and shattered hearts, we can (like Amy and thousands of others) survive this season of single parenting and be able to point back and say, "Look what the Lord has done."

In order to say that, however, we must first remember to keep our direction focused. Too often on a long journey I begin to ignore my GPS—even turning the volume down so I can hear the radio better. Before long I realize I've lost my way and must reestablish an effective route. When you find yourself there, don't lose heart, my friend. That's what recalculating is all about.

Keep Your Eyes on the Road

When I first found myself raising kids without a wife, it scared me. In survival mode I held on tight to the steering wheel and just drove. I didn't care where the road took me as long as I kept the car inside the lane markers. I understand how you might freak out. My friend, don't panic. Thousands of us dads have navigated this road before you. Single dads have traveled this path when all they had was a gravel road and a horse. We ride on their shoulders.

Mistakes will be made; count on it. A glance from time to time at your dashboard might eliminate some problems if you can catch them quick enough. But it's not the end of the world if you lose a belt. You just fix it and move on.

Still, sometimes we feel like mistakes are failures. We have this self-imposed pressure to appear invincible—refusing to admit (even to ourselves) we have weak areas in our lives. That can create some real problems for us superheroes.

For me, it's not mistakes—stress is my nemesis. If something makes me angry I stuff it down and move forward. If something emotional or sad occurs, I try to be stoic. When my schedule is overbooked and I haven't allowed enough cushion between major projects or deadlines, I keep going. After all, I can't appear to be fragile. The problem is I begin to forget things, even mid-sentence. That's the first warning sign. If I continue neglecting myself, the stress shows up physically.

I used to get chest pain and run to the emergency room thinking I was having a heart attack, only to have the doctors tell me my heart was very healthy and my issues were stress related. I finally understood what the doctor meant when I began to exercise and found the symptoms went away. I felt wonderful. Today, with the help of my attentive wife, I've learned to discern stress, and I'm able to change course before it overcomes me.

GRAB 'N GO

Meal assembly services that offer preplanned dinners are a new concept quickly becoming popular for busy single parents.

Simply find a center, decide your budget and how many to feed, then take home up to a month of meals.

Keeping ourselves physically, mentally, and emotionally healthy in the midst of stressors helps us with clearer decision-making skills when it comes to raising our children. Most of all, a robust spiritual condition ensures the Holy Spirit is clearly heard over all the noise of this world and what Satan throws at us fathers. First Timothy 4:8 says, "for while bodily training is of some value, godliness is of value in every way, as it holds promise for the present life and also for the life to come."

Parenting alone is distracting. Sometimes you're going to veer off the road God has for you—but there is grace. Place both hands on the wheel; keep heaven on the horizon and a prayer on your lips.

Intercession

Whether you have an antagonistic relationship with your children's mother or it's wonderful, there will be times when buttons are pushed and fires are lit that seem to dredge up all the godlessness inside you both. If you can't find it in you to pray for your ex, at least pray for your child.

One of the greatest, most efficient things we can do to help our child recover from a broken family is to pray for them. Yet so often we fail to stop and do this. One thing I struggled with was praying specifically. So when I intercede, I make a point of praying for certain things, not general blanket requests.

There's nothing more rewarding than seeing the Lord move in their lives as a result of prayer. So what should we pray for? Where do we start? How specific are we to pray? I'm hoping some of these ideas will help you.

- Pray your child would listen to God's voice and know his will for his or her life.
- Pray your child develops discernment and wisdom to choose godly friends and steer clear from those who might harm or deceive him.
- Pray your child would stay faithful to Christ until the end, study God's Word, and love the church.
- Ask the Lord to help your child stay sexually pure until marriage.
- Pray for your child's physical and emotional health during this difficult season of life.
- Pray your child would be released from any feelings that he or she caused the divorce.
- Ask for God's favor to be poured over your child and to assign angels to protect him or her.
- Pray for your child academically and socially.
- Pray your child will honor and obey his mother, being a blessing to her.

The power of a father's prayers is unbelievable. Prayer can be your child's lifeline. Know your child. How can you pray if you have no idea what's going on in his or her life? Talking to your children about their feelings can reveal much about how to best pray for your son or daughter.

Prodigals

I have prayed for my kids since before they were born. I tell them all the time that I pray for them. I often pray with them. Perhaps you're one of those fathers who has interceded for your kids until no tears are left. Is your son or daughter pursuing the world? Do they show no signs of walking with God? I can certainly understand your passion to see evidence of a changed life.

All Christian parents desire salvation for their children. The ultimate reason we exist is to glorify God, to have a relationship with him, to be with him forever in heaven. The thought of our kids not sharing this and being forever separated from us and God can throw us into a panic. It can drive us to pray dangerous prayers like, "Whatever it takes, Lord, bring them to you."

Yikes, be careful with that one.

As of the printing of this book, my two oldest children have chosen to believe in God, but have yet to walk closely in a deep relationship with him. I'd be lying if I didn't say this was hard for me as a full-time missionary coming from a long line of pastors, evangelists, missionaries, and Christian workers. It's a spiritual heritage they've chosen not to embrace, for now. There was a time when I had a recurring dream. I was on a train with my ticket, waiting for my children to board. But they chose not to board—waving goodbye from the platform, tickets in hand, as the train slowly departed. I often woke up weeping.

Today we respect each other and can talk openly about my desire to see them walk closer to God. Sharaya and Caleb were dedicated to the Lord as babies and raised in church, so they are children of the covenant. They know the truth and the Lord continues to show me how he's working in them to draw their hearts. So I continue to pray. I'm confident they will have a life-changing experience with Christ one day.

If you have children who tend to drift, continue to lift them up in prayer. God is faithful.

Dear Diary

Another way you can keep your destination in view is to write. I have a couple notebooks full of journals and records I kept during the years I was single fathering. Although many entries are filled with immature and embarrassing, emotion-laden raging, I found it helpful to look back and see how God had answered prayers. You may not be a journaling type of guy, but I recommend giving it a try for just five minutes each day. If not as a spiritual discipline during this season, then do it at least so you have a record of your thoughts that your kids can read someday when you have left this earth. It will be precious to them.

Beginning this splendid habit can be daunting, I know. All those blank, white pages are staring at you. You're wondering if it's really safe to put your thoughts or prayers in print.

I don't recommend using your computer. It's too easy in the heat of the moment to cut and post things you think others need to read. Much harder to do so using a real pen on a page. It's also too easy for you to return to the entry and edit it, erasing all the rawness of the moment. Try some of the following exercises to help get you started.

1. Make the first entry an introduction. Explain why you want to journal and what you hope to gain.
2. Switch it up. Some days you might feel like just writing to yourself. Other days you might write to God. Still other days you might make an entry to your child. There's no rule for how you share these thoughts. Nobody ever has to read them. It's more about getting those thoughts out of your head and on paper for your own growth. Doing this can also release that pressure valve of sadness or anger.
3. Just write. It might come out mundane at first, but at least you're making the ink flow. The more you write, the easier thoughts will begin flowing. If you can't get past your writer's block, write about your job, your spiritual journey, your childhood, the book you're reading, today's top news story, or even your death. What makes you irritable, happy, scared, calm, or desperate? The easiest entry for me is to ask myself, "What is God showing me today?" Any topic works as long as you're writing regularly.
4. Pour out your heart to God. You don't have to write down private thoughts and prayers. Especially if you're afraid your entries may get into the wrong hands. If you're not comfortable being frank,

then don't be. You're not a wimp if you decide to omit confessions of porn addiction or daydreams of your ex-wife's accidental death. Just write what you're comfortable writing.

5. Include your frustrations or victories specifically related to the divorce and your kids. These will be valuable to you one day as you review how God sustained you through it all. Those early entries will be a springboard for your future journals. Hindsight is a beautiful gift.

6. After about ninety days, go back and read some of your entries. Additionally, review some of the interactive portions in this book. Recording those responses is a type of journaling. How have things changed? Reflect on what the Lord has shown you and write it down.

Keeping Up Appearances

The temptation to look like you're on top of it all can be strong. When impressing others becomes your goal, you've not just lost your way; your headlights are off and the bridge is out.

I'm still learning that short of being a Stepford dad, it's virtually impossible to be the perfect parent. You'd think by the time Christine and I had our two youngest, I would have this parenting thing down pat. However, Jadyn and Anicah are nothing like my first two. These little girls are constantly teaching me things about fatherhood I hadn't learned with my older children. Raising kids is like owning electronics; just when you figure them out, something new comes along and you have to relearn everything.

Relearning changes a person too. One thing I really enjoy is raising these two youngest along with a wife—the way God planned it to be. I hadn't experienced much of this, and it's nothing less than lovely.

Yes, I used the word *lovely*. That's one consequence of living in an all-female household these days. Dare I mention how much I know about Barbie, mermaids, and fairies? I've grown soft around all this prettiness. Where's Caleb when I need him?

Whether you feel confident as a dad or not, people aren't really look-ing to be impressed by your fathering. I wasted a lot of energy worrying about what people thought about me. During the early years of single par-enting even my Christmas cards revealed some insecurity. They included the kids and me wearing dark sunglasses and sitting on a cool-looking balcony. After all, I had to keep up the image that I was fine and having fun. Remember the model cars—Jeep Dad, Hummer Dad, Convertible Dad, Minivan Dad, Clunker Dad, Electric Mini Dad, Model T Dad, and Sedan Dad—from chapter 10? I probably fell into each of those roles over the seven years I was fathering my kids alone. It wasn't until my Heavenly Father helped me see my true worth was in being myself that I finally became a Sedan.

Today I try not to deplete my energy on appearances. I care very little these days about what people think of me, allowing myself to be weak, transparent, and full of flaws so the Lord can show his glorious strength.

I trust this book in no way portrays me as someone who has it all together. I still tick off my grown kids when I get too preachy. I yell at my little girls until they cry. Sometimes I punish them so harshly I can almost see their little hearts curl up like a Styrofoam cup in a fire pit. I'm selfish, and I talk over them and get impatient when they can't express themselves. I get frustrated if they aren't fast enough. I complain when they break things and threaten never to buy them anything again. The list goes on.

I lie in bed and wonder how I can be so soft one day and so hard the next. How can I feel God using me sometimes to train them in the ways of the Lord, then turn around and in mere seconds let my flesh undo everything I taught them about God's love? Have I learned nothing about parenting kids? Are all four of my children destined to need counseling because of my stinkin' Tez-ness?

Then I see it. Those little eyes full of unfaltering love and admiration for me. Those sweet little smiles full of unconditional forgiveness. And that's Sharaya's and Caleb's faces.

I'm reminded of God's grace and mercy when I look at all four of my kids' faces. His love that covers a multitude of my sins. His love erases so many of my failures from my kids' minds and hearts. In my kids' eyes I see something that gives me hope.

Dads, you're going to goof up. We all do. Be encouraged in knowing you have a High Priest interceding for you. Your identity isn't in your shortcomings. It's in what you are becoming day by day by the transforming power of the Holy Spirit working in you, perfecting you, until one day you will be all he wants you to be.

Just Keep Swimming

In Disney Pixar's movie *Finding Nemo*, Marlin is a clownfish and single dad who coddles his only child. When Nemo is captured by some divers, Marlin crosses oceans searching for his lost son. As the fame of his heroic undertaking reaches his son in Sydney, Nemo finds the news astonishing and uncharacteristic of his dad. In the end he's reunited with a parent who has changed entirely. The crisis has transformed Marlin, making him a better father.

Trials have a way of reshaping all of us. In the midst of my own divorce no one could have convinced me that some good would have come out of that mess. I almost hesitate to say this because if you're in that place currently, chances are you aren't ready to hear this. But it's true. Each of us must wait for that period when God in his mercy reveals it to us—and he will. Good will rise from this tragedy, but you won't see it until, like Marlin, you reach your own Sydney. After you've made it through all the jellyfish, sharks, deep sea creatures, whales, and nets—then you'll be able to look back over that ocean of trouble and see how the Lord has sustained and changed you.

It happens in small increments, too tiny to notice. Adjustments here and modifications there. My friend Ernesto was fifty-one when he and his three teens found themselves in a broken home. As he adjusted to life apart from his children, he often panicked when he discovered special moments were occurring without his presence.

"I had to learn to focus on the big picture, not think about the small stuff," Ernesto admits. "My teens also had to develop a big-picture mentality."

FATHERHOOD SCARS
Discover why scars are precious.

When it was all said and done, Ernesto came out the other side a more godly man, a guy who hopes in Christ more now because the Lord changed his worry to trust. Sometimes God tweaks you like he did Ernesto, so slightly you don't notice until years down the road. Other times he makes huge, uncomfortable adjustments in a short amount of time, like Marlin experienced. You may not yet see the big picture, but rest in the understanding that God has you.

The World Atlas

Too often I get stuck on a city map, forgetting to study the atlas under the car seat. I need a bigger picture, a bird's-eye view to remind me where I'm headed. Keeping the destination in sight during our journey helps maintain perspective for what we're doing—for what will matter in heaven. We need an eternal outlook to avoid getting caught up in this world's temporal nonsense. You're going to face challenges that neither this book nor someone's cautionary advice will ever prepare you for. Your heart might break for your children as you see them take paths you didn't want them to take. You may need to forgive someone a thousand times for hurting you. Regret and guilt may overcome you, tempting you to blame yourself for other people's choices. It's paralyzing when all you can see are the mountain walls around your valley. You need a bird's-eye view to remind you this too will pass. Pull back from that little map and open the atlas.

The Lord has granted you one of the greatest honors—to be a daddy. So take heart, the Heavenly Father loves you and has a wonderful plan for those he calls his own.

CHECKING YOUR GAUGES

Was there a section in this book that ticked you off? Why is that?

What have you done to help yourself become physically, mentally, and spiritually healthier?

In what areas do you feel most lost as a single parent? What are you doing to better navigate those areas?

STUDYING THE MAP

"Thus says the LORD, who makes a way in the sea, a path in the mighty waters . . . : 'Remember not the former things, nor consider the things of old. Behold, I am doing a new thing; now it springs forth, do you not perceive it? I will make a way in the wilderness and rivers in the desert.'" Isaiah 43:16, 18–19

REROUTING

Which chapter in this book challenged you most? Reread it and ask God to reveal his will for you on that topic.

If you've skipped over any of the interactive sections at the end of each chapter, go back and complete them. Consider memorizing some of the Scripture passages.

Pass this book along to another single dad you know. Better yet, buy him his own copy.

REFUELING

Father, thank you for my children. Show me what they need most from me as a daddy. I know I can't meet my children's every need. Only you can do that. But help me to be a sensitive protector of my kids. Sometimes it's hard to be both. Give me the energy to care for them properly and ears to listen, so that I may know them in a deeper way. Bind us close with cords that can't be broken. Bless my ex-wife in every way. Draw her ever closer to your heart, Father. Help me to model love and forgiveness toward her. Finally, teach me to be fun in the midst of this tiring job of raising my children in this wicked world. Make my home a warm, safe place where they feel the presence of your Holy Spirit. In Christ's holy name, amen.

Postcards from the Road
(Wisdom from Other Road Warriors)

"You know you could lose your driver's license for that."

We all need to know we're not alone as single fathers. We often don't get a chance as men to gather and share our failures, our wisdom, advice, and creative ideas. Here's a collection of memories from dads as they recall their own road trips.

On Childproofing Your Home

My son was three. I woke up late one morning shortly after his mom and I divorced. I walked into the living room to find him sitting quietly in the middle of the floor with two pounds of fresh coffee grounds piled up in front of him. I asked him what he was doing. "Making a castle," he responded with a tone that suggested I was silly to ask about the obvious. Lesson one: don't oversleep.

— Tom (California)

On Cooking

Chili too hot for the kids? Add a spoonful of peanut butter to calm the heat. If your chili or spaghetti sauce is too acidic, add a sliced carrot to neutralize the acid. Boring lunches? Use large cookie cutters to turn sandwiches into fun shapes. Your kids might like it too.

—Cam (Florida)

I keep a list of favorite foods, snacks, sweets for each of my kids. Then I surprise them by buying or cooking for them. Sometimes I tuck their favorite candy into their lunch bag. While I'm at it, I include a little note to encourage them.

—Ke (Singapore)

NEW DADDIES
For tips on how to hold, burp, and diaper your infant.

On Praying for Your Kids

I remember as if it was yesterday. While her mother recovered, the nurses let me give my baby her first bath. As I sponged off the tiny little fingers and toes I snuck little kisses from time to time. What was God thinking? I wasn't qualified. I had no idea how to nurture a girl. I grew up in an all-male house, so I was pretty much raised by wolves. I prayed over her and at that moment I began praying for her future husband too—a prayer that continues today.

— Antwon (Michigan)

On Securing a Better Life for Your Kid

If you want your child to make better choices, those choices have to be there for them to pick from. Some choices aren't even there in certain environments, so a kid can't even choose. I made sacrifices—had to. We sold this huge house in the country and relocated to the suburbs. It was a smaller home in a nicer neighborhood. Then I placed the kids in a private school. These changes opened up a whole new set of opportunities I never had as a kid. By exposing my children to more affluent people, it helped them set their sights higher for their education, careers, and their future spouses.

—Craig (Michigan)

Travel with your kids, throughout the United States and overseas. Meeting people and making friends from other places is an awesome learning experience. Exposing them to different cultures enriches them in ways I never could. Travel enlarges their world to things and instills a sense of adventure. It removes fear from the equation, making an impossible opportunity seem normal as they reach adulthood. You'll find your child may backpack across America, study abroad, go on a mission trip, or accept that high-paying job offer in Japan. You'll just shake your head and say, "Why didn't I do that when I was their age?"

10 TIPS FOR COURT

1. Arrive early.
2. Dress conservatively.
3. Be prepared—have documentation.
4. Be courteous to court staff.
5. Turn off the cell phone. No gum.
6. Keep a poker face.
7. Be clear and confident.
8. Show interest.
9. Know when to shut up.
10. Memorize this list.

—TJ (Texas)

On Discipline

I often found a good spanking (when done in love, not anger) drew my child's heart toward me. For the rest of the day they became the most wonderful child a human could ask for, every time. I'm convinced the boundaries that are spotlighted as a result of discipline make children feel loved and protected. Still yet, don't depend on this alone to convey your love. They need to hear you say you love them daily.

—Carey (Alabama)

On Child Support

One of the best decisions I made was to request my child support be automatically deducted from my paycheck. This ensured a detailed court record of every timely deposit I made. My extra payments were recorded too, creating a large credit. The records proved invaluable when I had to defend myself in court one day.

—Cam (Florida)

On Quality Time

I found that successful bedtime was all about routine. That meant reading to my kids almost every night. They came to expect it, and it represented something they could count on, regardless of what might have happened during the day.

—Denny (Kentucky)

Keeping in touch with what's going on in their world is key. That's difficult in my line of work. I deal with adults who expect things fast and well organized. You can't bring that home when dealing with your kids. They are not a business unit and they are not efficient. You have to get on the floor with them and be a part of their world. So you kind of have to waste some time being inefficient. They might want to build a balloon made out of lead. But you have to give them time to learn a lesson you already have the answer to.

—Brad (New Zealand)

On the Emerging Faith of Your Child

Be in the moment with your kids. Not instructing, directing, or parenting, but in the moment of whatever they are doing. In the middle of those moments there are often life issues/scenarios that bleed out of simple conversation, which I am able to bandage with God's truth. I've found that those are very rich moments of grace.

— Cooper (Florida)

It's important I keep an open relationship with my teen, remembering to guide rather than nag. But at times I have to require things in order to be a good steward of the family God gave me. For instance, church attendance is not a choice for my teens to decide. I've made that decision for them and they must attend. If my parents didn't force me to go to church, I probably wouldn't be in ministry today. I'm not the perfect parent; I make mistakes. Yet God has blessed me. My kids are now entering the ministry themselves.

—Ricky (Italy)

We so often expect immediate change, but God has his own timing. I find the challenge to be inside me. I have to stay true to God's timing, not my own. So I pray for patience.

—Hector (Florida)

Be real and transparent about your brokenness, especially as they get to be older teens. In the end every kid makes his own choices. All you can do is try, but free will is always there. Knowing that releases me from potential guilt trips.

—Brad (Florida)

On Daughters and Puberty

My thirteen-year-old daughter and I are very close. One day I took her to Urgent Care with flu symptoms. She laid her head on my shoulder in the waiting room. Our turn eventually came and the doctor began asking questions pertaining to her health. The subject of menstrual cycles came up and she looked at me with an I-don't-want-to-discuss-this-in-front-of-my-father look. I had to laugh. We have had very open and honest conversations about faith, forgiveness, and our relationship with Christ. Up until then we forgot to discuss periods. That day I learned the importance of discussing subjects we might normally shy away from. Being open (within reason) and having a mature conversation helps build a tighter bond between father and daughter and

ultimately solidifies trust for
more fragile topics.
—Donald (Louisiana)

"I think a dad has to make his
daughter feel that he's genuinely
interested in what she's going
through."
—Harry Connick Jr.[1]

On Teen Daughters

My three girls were a mess of
hormones, relationships, anxieties, and sweetness. What a confusing time of life for them. I had to listen to everything and hear
their hearts in order to connect. Just hanging with or going on
dates with them helped us talk through stuff—including sex and
what guys are after. It helped when I opened up about my own
personal failures, marriage struggles, and sinful desires.

—Jake (Ohio)

On Visitation

For my ex and me, seeing each other's living arrangements stirred
up unhealthy responses. So I began exchanging the kids in a neu-
tral location. I was careful not to schedule the swap at my beloved
restaurant or park. I chose a stark, empty parking lot or some foul
location I knew I would never go for recreation. The last thing
I wanted was to feel nauseated every time I went there over the
next one hundred years, remembering all those dreaded drop-
offs peppered with infuriating arguments. Think ahead; don't
ruin your favorite hangouts with sad memories—boundaries are
good.

—Reece (Florida)

All kids need a dad who is present and actively involved in their
lives as best you can—even if they shut you out. You try, you call,
you send texts. You talk about them and to them. They need to
know you haven't placed them on a shelf but on your mind daily.

—Dan (Minnesota)

On Blended Siblings

We never used the word *half* in reference to our children as siblings. When outsiders use the word, we quickly correct them too. They are brothers and sisters, period. The word *half* alludes to division or separation by assigning levels of importance. Our children are not half of anything.

— Lou (Florida)

On Sex Education

One day my seven-year-old son and I were walking through a science center and came upon life-sized figures of Neanderthals—male and female. They were nude and the genitals were too prominent to ignore. Rather than avoid the topic I turned it into an opportunity to teach my son anatomy. "You see this, Son? This is called a vagina and the penis over here fits inside it perfectly." The lesson went on, but you get the point. It took all the mystery and taboo out of the equation and made future discussions much easier.

—Devon (Florida)

On Your Child's Virginity

When my son was twelve we went camping and listened to some CDs on puberty and the treasure of virginity. We had some frank discussions about saving yourself for marriage and I felt like it was a real bonding time. But later I found out he had already been molested by an older girl and was afraid to tell me. Porn became a problem for him. I felt like my heart was gonna burst with grief. More because he felt for some reason I wasn't a safe enough person to tell. I suppose I needed to begin those sex conversations much earlier, but who knew twelve years old was too late.

—Randy (North Carolina)

On Mobile Devices

Technology gives a substantial amount of freedom to our children. Suddenly at the tip of their fingers is a vast amount of information. Unsupervised they are able to learn things well beyond their years. My son was nine when he insisted he needed an online mobile device. Are you kidding me? Sometimes we want to do nice things for our children but often forget the responsibility that comes with these entitlements we afford them. I believe it's critically important to teach our children boundaries and the differences between what's good and what's not good online.

—Jay (Louisiana)

On Meeting the Other Man

With all his interactions with the kids, he and I finally decided to meet over coffee. He wanted to shake my hand. I ignored it and began talking business about what not to do in front of the kids—ya know, no drinking, cussing, or making out with their mother. He was younger than me and a little jittery, so I felt superior. For a short time. In the end, I felt humiliated—after all, he was the one who went home each night to my wife. It didn't last long; they broke up. It's been six years and I'm still meeting with these men. They come and go—my kids don't even blink.

—Andy (Virginia)

On Movies and Television

I found how important it was to be sure my kids could handle media content both intellectually and emotionally. I remember a few times when my kids were about seven and ten years old I allowed them to watch some movies and television shows that were too mature for them, because they had always acted more mature than their ages. Then I learned of some nightmare issues and bedtime anxieties my daughter was having. That taught me a lesson. There is a difference between how children act versus how they feel. I failed to realize my daughter's intellectual maturity differed from her emotional maturity. Virtually all of her life's crises have stemmed from that wide gap. When setting movie and television boundaries, remember it's not just about a child's age or vocabulary.

—John (Texas)

On Dating

I met alone with the boys that wanted to court my daughters. We used that time to get to know each other. I remember telling them, "I don't know you well enough to lend you my car; why should I lend you my daughter?" We spent time together as a family too. Eventually I allowed them time alone, after I was convinced my girl was safe with them.

—Wes (Florida)

The boys started noticing my teenage daughter, and when she started dating I wanted to lock her up in the basement. One time her heart was broken by this guy, and it killed me that I wasn't there. The phone just isn't enough sometimes. I wanted to reach through the phone lines and just hug her. Other times I wanted to fly out with a baseball bat and take care of some of her boy problems for her.

—Steve (Colorado)

On Your Child's Wedding

Teach [your child] that marriage is a holy bond meant to last until death. Regardless of the divorce. That they should never take [their] vows to God and each other lightly. This is one of the most sober, serious, God-fearing unions we as humans can ever make. It won't always be fun. Some mornings they'll wake up and just not feel very in love with each other. There will be times they feel like giving up. They need to know love is not a feeling; it's a choice, every day.

— Joel (Michigan)

On Surviving in General

God is big. He created the universe with only his words. He is on your side so you and your family will always prevail. You never know how strong you are until being strong in the Lord is all you have left.

—Barry (Minnesota)

Notes

Introduction: So Why a Book?

1. Quoted in Gracie Bonds Staples, "More Single Dads in Charge," June 15, 2011, *The Atlanta Journal-Constitution*, http://www.ajc.com/news/lifestyles/more-single-dads-in-charge/nQwQh/.

Chapter 1: Where in the World Am I?

1. Carey Casey, "Being a Father Is a Great Privilege and Responsibility," January 2, 2014, Fathers.com, National Center for Fathering, http://fathers.com/being-a-father-is-a-great-privilege-and-responsibility.
2. Adapted from Andy Harrelson, "How Not to Become Your Absentee Father," March 15, 2013, The Art of Manliness, http://www.artofmanliness.com/2013/03/15/how-not-to-become-your-absentee-father/.
3. David Hochman, "Q&A with William Shatner," accessed March 17, 2014, http://www.details.com/celebrities-entertainment/men-of-the-moment/200712/wiseguy-sci-fi-and-star-trek-legend-william-shatner.
4. Emily V. Gordon, "Quick Remarriages, Gender, and How We Treat Our Divorcées," January 20, 2011, *The Huffington Post*, www.huffingtonpost.com/emily-gordon/quick-remarriages-gender-_b_811815.html.

Chapter 2: Who's Driving?

1. Shana Schutte, "Trusting: Let God Do the Driving," 2009, *Focus on the Family* magazine, www.focusonthefamily.com/faith/faith_in_life/risking/trusting.aspx.

2. Amanda Lenhart, Rich Ling, Scott Campbell, and Kristen Pur-
cell, "Teens and Mobile Phones," April 20, 2010, Pew Research
Internet Project, www.pewinternet.org/2010/04/20/teens-and-mo
bile-phones/.

3. Amanda Lenhart, "Teens and Sexting," December 15, 2009, Pew
Research Internet Project, www.pewinternet.org/2009/12/15/teens
-and-sexting/.

4. Gwenn Schurgin O'Keeffe and Kathleen Clarke-Pearson, "The
Impact of Social Media on Children, Adolescents, and Families,"
Pediatrics 127, no. 4 (April 1, 2011), doi: 10.1542/peds.2011-0054.

5. Cox Communications and National Center for Missing and
Exploited Children, "Teen Online and Wireless Safety Survey on
Cyberbullying, Sexting and Parental Controls," May 2009, ww2
.cox.com/wcm/en/aboutus/datasheet/takecharge/2009-teen-survey
.pdf.

6. Chris Heath, "Mr. Hannah Montana's Achy Broken Heart,"
March 2011, *GQ*, www.gq.com/entertainment/celebrities/201103
/billy-ray-cyrus-mr-hannah-montana-miley.

Chapter 3: The Engine Lights

1. GAO/HRD-92-39FS, January 9, 1992, and DHHS Greenbook,
chapter 11, quoted in "Child Support Statistics" 2008, Father Focus
Inc., http://www.fatherfocus.net/index-5.html.

2. WZAK, "20 Breakup Statistics That Show We Aren't Over Our Ex,"
February 4, 2011, http://wzakcleveland.com/1888141/20-breakup
-statistics-that-show-we-arent-over-our-exes/.

Chapter 4: A Fork in the Road

1. Mayo Clinic Staff, "Forgiveness: Letting Go of Grudges and Bitterness," November 23, 2011, http://www.mayoclinic.org/healthy
-living/adult-health/in-depth/forgiveness/art-20047692?pg=1.

2. Tez Brooks, *Somewhere in the Journey* (self published, 2004).

Chapter 7: Regular Tune-Ups, Part 2

1. Mike Klumpp, *The Single Dad's Survival Guide* (Colorado Springs: Waterbrook Press, 2003), 22.
2. D. L. Moody, *Prevailing Prayer: What Hinders It?* (Chicago: F. H. Revell, 1884), 61.

Chapter 8: Prepping the Motor Home

1. Jared Diamond, "Animal Art: Variation in Bower Decorating Style Among Male Bowerbirds *Amblyornis inornatus*," *Proc. Natl. Acad. Sci. USA* 83 (May 1986): 3046, http://www.pnas.org/content/83/9/3042.full.pdf.

Chapter 10: Model Cars

1. OWN [Oprah Winfrey Network], "Absent Fathers: An Absentee Dad Explains Why Men Leave Their Children," May 8, 2013, Huffington Post, http://www.huffingtonpost.com/2013/05/08/absent-fathers-dad-why-men-leave-children_n_3231932.html.
2. Edward T. Welch, *When People Are Big and God Is Small* (Phillipsburg, NJ: P&R Publishing, 1997), chapter 1.
3. Joy Behar Show, "Interview with Dave Ramsey" August 15, 2011, transcript, http://transcripts.cnn.com/transcripts/1108/15/joy.01.html.
4. Doris J. James, "Profile of Jail Inmates, 2002," U.S. Department of Justice, Bureau of Justice Statistics Special Report, p. 9, revised October 12, 2004, http://www.bjs.gov/content/pub/pdf/pji02.pdf.
5. Will Welch, "Eminem," *GQ*, 2011, http://www.gq.com/entertainment/music/201111/survivors-music-portfolio-eminem-rap.
6. Quoted in "Countdown to the Canonizations of Blessed John XXIII & Blessed John Paul II: A Commentary by Father Richard Kunst: Soon-to-Be Saints Left Us Words of Wisdom," April 12, 2014, Papal Artifacts, http://www.papalartifacts.com/post/877.

Chapter 13: Selling the Minivan

1. Susan Yara, "Father's Empty Nest," August 23, 2006, Forbes, www
   .forbes.com/2006/08/22/empty-nest-men_cx_sy_0823dads.html.

Chapter 15: A Two-Car Garage

1. Jackie Morgan MacDougall, "7 Tips to Save Your Marriage . . .
   From the Kids," March 26, 2013, Huffington Post. Retrieved from
   www.huffingtonpost.com/jackie-morgan-macdougall/7-tips-to
   -save-your-marri_b_2909724.html.
2. Ron L. Deal, "Placing Your Spouse in the 'Front Seat' of Your
   Heart," FamilyLife, accessed April 16, 2014, www.familylife.com
   /articles/topics/blended-family/remarriage/staying-married/placing
   -your-spouse-in-the-front-seat-of-your-heart#.Ur3mYOpdVfy.

Chapter 16: Taking the Bus

1. Sarah Kinbar, "Blended Families," *Playground Magazine* (Fall 2013).
2. Theodore Roosevelt, speech to the Holy Name Society, Oyster Bay,
   New York, August 16, 1903, accessed April 16, 2014, www.theodore
   -roosevelt.com/images/research/txtspeeches/86.txt.

Chapter 17: The Less Familiar Route

1. Interview by DeMarco Williams, "National (Guilty) Pleasure,"
   INsite, accessed April 16, 2014, http://www.insiteatlanta.com
   /nicholascage.asp.

Epilogue: Postcards from the Road

1. April Rueb, "Interview: Harry Connick, Jr., His Daughter, and Their
   'American Girl' Collaboration," *Parents* magazine, September 12,
   2011, www.parents.com/blogs/goodyblog/2011/09/interview-with
   -harry-connick-jr-american-girls-collaboration/.